the CARTOONISTS CLUB

RAINA TELGEMEIER & SCOTT McCLOUD

the CARTOONISTS CLUB

graphix

An Imprint of

SCHOLASTIC

INKING BY **RAY BAEHR**

COLOR BY **BENIAM C. HOLLMAN**

LETTERING BY **JESSE POST**

Library of Congress Control Number: 2024936812

ISBN 978-93-5954-149-5

Printed in India at: VK Global Digital Private Limited
This reprint edition, August 2025

Edited by Cassandra Pelham Fulton
Creative Director: Phil Falco
Publisher: David Saylor

ATH

CHAPTER ONE

Beep Beep
Beee-
6:45
WHACK!

MMM. JUST FIVE MORE MINUTES.
MAKAYLA, HURRY UP!
KNOCK KNOCK
EEEP!
7:19
Brush Brush
Brush Brush

COMING!!
CARPOOL'S HERE! LOVE YOU!
munch munch munch
LOVE **YOU.** WHERE ARE MY KEYS?
HEY, MOM! I THOUGHT UP A NEW CHARACTER FOR MY --
LATER, HONEY!
I CALL FRONT SEAT.
COATS ON, EVERYONE!
VROOOOM
DID YOU FINISH YOUR HOMEWORK?
I GOT TO LEVEL **SIX** LAST NIGHT!
GENE, DID YOU REMEMBER TO HAVE YOUR MOM SIGN YOUR PERMISSION SLIP?
...OH NO!

CRAFT
MIDDLE SCH
3:33

NOW, REMEMBER OUR ORDER OF OPERATIONS ...
MULTIPLICATION AND DIVISION COME BEFORE ADDITION AND SUBTRACTION, SO IN THIS CASE ...
5 x 7 + 13 =
Which comes first
Operations
6x+15
YOU'LL WANT TO MULTIPLY 5 TIMES 7 FIRST ...
Tap
Tap
AND THEN ADD THE 13 ...

HOWARD, WE'RE NOT SUPPOSED TO --
SO, 5 TIMES 7 EQUALS . . . ANYONE?
5 x 7 + 13 =
35!
GOOD, JILLIAN. 35 PLUS 13 FOR A TOTAL OF . . .
Mr Rugget
2 + 2 =
blah blah blah blah

KPT HPFLT!
Mr Rugget
2 + 2 =
blah blah
blah blah blah
blah blah
blah blah blah blah
ZZZZZ
student
Hee
Hee
Hee
Hee
Hee

NOW, ON THE OTHER HAND, IF 7 PLUS 13 WAS IN PARENTHESES . . .
Tap
Hee
Hee
Hee
Hee
HOWARD? MAKAYLA? ANYTHING YOU'D LIKE TO SHARE WITH THE REST OF THE CLASS?
NO, MR. RUGGETT. SORRY.
SEE ME AFTER CLASS, PLEASE. BOTH OF YOU.

RINNNG!
HOWARD, THIS IS THE THIRD TIME THIS WEEK THAT YOU'VE DISRUPTED MY LESSONS!
I KNOW YOU LIKE TO DRAW, BUT ...
CAN YOU PLEASE WAIT UNTIL **AFTER** ALGEBRA TO DO SO?

YES. SORRY.
AND, MAKAYLA . . .
IF HOWARD IS BOTHERING YOU, I CAN MOVE YOU TO A DIFFERENT SEAT.
NO!
PLEASE DON'T.
I PROMISE WE WON'T MAKE ANY MORE TROUBLE!
EXIT
HOWARD, THAT WAS AN **AMAZING** DRAWING.

CAN I SEE IT AGAIN?
SURE!
IT'S IN MY BACKPACK. HERE, HOLD THIS.
ZIP
...
KSSHH!

HOWARD! OH MY GOSH.
THESE ARE...
WAIT! DON'T LOOK!
WHOA -- LOOK AT THIS! A CAT ON A BIKE! A WHALE IN A TOP HAT? I LOVE IT!!
I am King of WORLD!
SO STRWONG!
I Get ALL THE MONEY
I Hate Goodness.
OH NOES! HE IS A BAD APPLE!
THAT ONE'S NOT VERY GOOD...

THEY'RE GREAT!!
YOU THINK SO?!
OH! HERE'S MR. RUGGETT. HEE HEE!
YOU NAILED THE EXPRESSION.
DO YOU WRITE STORIES, TOO?
I DON'T HAVE ANY STORY IDEAS.
WHAT?!
munch

BUT ... YOU HAVE MILLIONS OF FUNNY DRAWINGS!
STORIES ARE HARD.
SERIOUSLY?! THAT'S THE **EASY** PART FOR ME!
I THINK OF NEW STORY IDEAS ALL DAY LONG!
I'M WORKING ON A BIG STORY FOR MY OWN SERIES THAT HAS A GALACTIC PRINCESS AND A FLYING UNICORN ARMY AND GIANT SPACESHIPS ...
COOL!

I WRITE EVERYTHING DOWN IN THESE IDEA NOTEBOOKS. I'VE FILLED THREE OF THEM SO FAR THIS YEAR.
HAVE YOU READ *BATTLE PRINCESS KISHIMOTO?*
YOUR STORY SOUNDS A LITTLE LIKE THAT STORY.
ARE YOU KIDDING?! I **LOVE** *BATTLE PRINCESS KISHIMOTO!*
ME TOO!!
SOOOOOOO GOOD!!!
MY STORY IS TOTALLY DIFFERENT, THOUGH.
MAKAYLA . . .

COULD YOU MAYBE ... HELP ME COME UP WITH A STORY FOR MY DRAWINGS?
I MEAN ... WHERE DO YOU GET YOUR IDEAS?
I DON'T KNOW. FROM EVERYWHERE, I GUESS? I JUST LOOK AROUND AND PICK SOMETHING.
HMM ...
DO YOU THINK I COULD MAKE A STORY OUT OF THIS CHICKEN NUGGET?
SURE!

HE'S AN EEEEVIL CHICKEN NUGGET WHO, UM ...
OH! OH! WHO WEARS A DIFFERENT DIPPING SAUCE OUTFIT EVERY DAY!
THAT'S THE IDEA!
dip
AND HIS ARCHENEMY COULD BE THIS TOFU DOG!
YEAH!
"THAT'S THE LAST TIME YOU FOOL **ME,** CHICKENNNNNN!"
"IF 5 TIMES 7 WAS INSIDE THE PARENTHESES ..."

BAHAHAHAHAHA!!!
THE NUGGET IS A MATH TEACHER!!
RUGGETT RHYMES WITH NUGGET!
THIS CAN BE HIS DOG, TOFU PUP.
NO, TOFU PUP IS HIS ENEMY, RIGHT?
WHICH MEANS TOFU PUP IS ACTUALLY A HERO . . .
MUNCH
BUT OUR STORY IS FROM MR. NUGGET'S POINT OF VIEW, SO --
AUGH!
YOU'RE EATING THE HERO!
IT'S MY LUNCH!
HA HA HA HA HA HA HA HA HA HA HA

CAFETERIA
HEE HEE
CRA
MIDDLE
I GUESS WE CAN'T JUST PLAY WITH OUR FOOD TO MAKE UP STORIES.
TOFU PUP HAS INSPIRED ME...
MEET ME IN THE LIBRARY AFTER SCHOOL, OKAY?
I HAVE AN IDEA.

CHAPTER TWO

EARTH
& SKY
NEW
PLATO
ATE MY SNACK
HEY!
i ♥ bugs

creeeeeeeeeeeak...
SLAM!
LIBRARY
Blah
Blah
Blah
Blah
Blah
Blah
Blah
Blah
Blah
Blah
Blah

BLAH BLAH BLAH BLAH BLAH BLAH BLAH BLAH BLAH BLAH BLAH BLAH BLAH MR. RUGGETT BLAH BLAH BLAH BLAH BLAH BLAH BLAH BLAH BLAH BLAH BLAH BLAH BLAH BLAH BLAH BLAH BLAH BLAH BLAH BLAH BLAH BLAH BLAH BLAH BLAH BLAH BLAH LUNCHTIME . . . BLAH BLAH BLAH BLAH BLAH BLAH BLAH BLAH BLAH BLAH BLAH BLAH BLAH BLAH BLAH BLAH BLAH BLAH BLAH BLAH
Blah Blah Blah Blah
Blah Blah Blah Blah Blah Blah
BLAH BLAH BLAH BLAH BLAH BLAH BLAH BLAH BLAH BLAH BLAH BLAH BLAH BLAH BLAH BLAH BLAH BLAH BLAH BLAH BLAH BLAH COMICS . . .

OKAY, SO WE'VE GOT A HERO AND A VILLAIN ...
I'LL START DESIGNING THEM.
HMM ...
B.B.Q.
CHICKEN NUGGETS ARE KIND OF SHAPELESS, AREN'T THEY?
CAN YOU PUT A CHICKEN FACE ON IT?
OR MAYBE A FACE LIKE MR. RUGGETT'S?
HOW ABOUT **BOTH?**
HA HA
HA HA
B.B.Q.

CAN HE ALSO HAVE CHICKEN LEGS?
EASY.
B.B.Q.
HA HA HA! IT MAKES NO SENSE AT ALL!
I KNOW!!
HA HA HA HA HA HA HA HA HA
HA HA HA HA HA HA
chuckle
"CURSE YOU, TOFU PUP!"
B.B.Q.
"HANDS OFF THOSE KIDS, EVIL NUGGET!"

Heh...
Ha Ha...
Sigh.
SO WHAT'S THE STORY, THEN?
I CAN WRITE THE FIRST ONE.
Once upon a time there was a chicken nugget. But not just any chicken nugget... a super-evil villain math teacher chicken nugget.
TEN MINUTES LATER
wheeeze
COOL, BUT ... THIS IS A STORY THAT YOU **WROTE.** HOW DO WE TURN IT INTO A COMIC?
groan

TEN MORE MINUTES LATER
HERE YOU GO! I BROKE UP THE STORY INTO CHUNKS AND COPIED THE WORDS INTO PANEL BOXES THAT YOU CAN DRAW IN . . .
① Once upon a time there was a chicken nugget.
② But not just any chicken nugget... a super-evil villain math teacher chicken nugget.
③ One day, he went to school in his car wearing his favorite BBQ pants...
④ On the way he was thinking of all kinds of mean tests he could give the students...
⑤ When he sees Tofu Pup flying overhead, he gets an evil idea.
⑥ If that cursed Tofu Dog doesn't leave me alone, I'll—
UM, OKAY, BUT IT DOESN'T LEAVE MUCH ROOM FOR THE ART PART.
SO DRAW REALLY SMALL!
OR . . . WRITE FEWER WORDS!

OR . . . COMPROMISE!
SORRY, DIDN'T MEAN TO INTERRUPT. I'M MS. FATIMA, THE SCHOOL LIBRARY'S MEDIA SPECIALIST.
DID I HEAR THAT YOU'RE WORKING ON A COMIC TOGETHER?
UH-HUH!
WE JUST STARTED!
I LOVE COMICS! IN FACT, I'M THE ONE WHO ORDERS ALL THE COMICS AND GRAPHIC NOVELS FOR THE LIBRARY.
HAVE YOU READ *BATTLE PRINCESS KISHIMOTO*??
ONLY UP TO VOLUME EIGHT. THERE'S A HOLD LIST A MILE LONG FOR THE REST OF THE VOLUMES.

VOLUME EIGHT IS THE BEST!
SOOOOOO GOOD!
I'D LIKE TO HEAR ABOUT **YOUR** COMIC! DOES IT HAVE A STORY YET?
YES!
I MEAN, SORT OF.
ANCIENT WORLD
DINOS
Read!
I'M HELPING HOWARD WITH THE STORY, AND HE'S DONE SOME GREAT DRAWINGS...
BUT IT FEELS LIKE THE WORDS AND THE PICTURES ARE KIND OF **FIGHTING** EACH OTHER.

SO WHICH COMES FIRST IN COMICS?
THE **PICTURES** OR THE **WORDS?**
WELL, IN COMICS, YOU WANT THE PICTURES AND WORDS TO WORK **TOGETHER** TO TELL STORIES.
BUT WHERE DO WE START? DO WE WRITE A SCRIPT OR JUST START DRAWING?
ALSO, HOW DO YOU WRITE A SCRIPT? AND WHAT'S THE RIGHT KIND OF PAPER?
WHAT KIND OF PEN OR BRUSH SHOULD I USE?
WELL ...
AND WHAT IF WE WANT TO PRINT IT?
LIBRARY

THESE ARE ALL GREAT QUESTIONS!
I THINK I KNOW SOME OF THE ANSWERS, BUT I'LL DO A LITTLE RESEARCH FOR YOU, TOO.
THANKS!!
IS THERE ANYTHING ELSE?
ACTUALLY, YES.
IT'S WHY WE CAME HERE TODAY ... WE WANT TO START A **CLUB** FOR KIDS WHO MAKE COMICS!
WE DO?

I MEAN, YEAH, WE DO!!
WELL, YOU'RE IN THE RIGHT PLACE. WE HAVE SPACE AFTER SCHOOL ON WEDNESDAYS!
WHAT WOULD YOU LIKE TO **CALL** YOUR CLUB?
OH ...
BOOKS
UM, THE KIDS-WHO-MAKE-COMICS CLUB? COMICS-MAKING CLUB? FOR ... UM ... NO ...
WHAT DO YOU EVEN **CALL** PEOPLE WHO WRITE AND DRAW COMICS?

A LOT OF PEOPLE JUST CALL THEM **CARTOONISTS.**
"THE CARTOONISTS CLUB"?
OOH, I LIKE IT.
the CARTOONISTS CLUB
CAN WE MAKE FLYERS?
LET'S GET STARTED!
Read!

AN HOUR LATER
ALL ARE WELCOME HERE
Read!
I'LL NEED TO LOCK UP SOON, LYNDA.
OKAY.
DO YOU THINK YOU'D EVER LIKE TO JOIN A CLUB LIKE THAT?
Shfff
I KNOW HOW MUCH YOU LOVE TO DRAW.
CAN I SEE WHAT YOU DREW TODAY?

NO WORRIES. YOU DON'T HAVE TO SHOW ME. SEE YOU TOMORROW?
MHM.
Announcing
THE CARTOONISTS CLUB!
I LOVE COMICS
EXIT
LIBRARY
CLICK

CHAPTER THREE

Announcing
THE CARTOONISTS CLUB!
Wednesdays at 3:15pm in the Craft Middle School Library.
I LIKE COMICS!
ME TOO!
ME TOO!
LET'S FORM A CLUB!
Questions? See Ms. Fatima!

THE FOLLOWING WEDNESDAY
WHAT IF NO ONE SHOWS UP? WHAT IF NO ONE SHOWS UP?!?
IT'S ONLY 3:10, MAKAYLA.
CLICK
HI, MS. FATIMA.
HI, LYNDA.

OH ... IT'S THE GIRL THAT'S HERE ALL THE TIME.
MAYBE SHE'LL JOIN OUR CLUB!
... OR MAYBE NOT.
GRAPHIC NOVELS
SHE **DOES** LIKE COMICS, IT SEEMS!
MAYBE SHE THINKS THAT'S WHAT THE CARTOONISTS CLUB IS! JUST READING!
I MEAN, **WE** LIKE READING COMICS, TOO, SO --
CLICK--
HELLO?

HI, IS THIS WHERE WE MEET FOR THE CARTOONIS--
HIIIII! YES! THAT'S US!
I'M MAKAYLA!!
HI! I'M ART. I USE THEY/THEM PRONOUNS.
OH!
I USE SHE/HER. I SHOULD HAVE TOLD YOU THAT RIGHT AWAY.
HI, MAKAYLA!
HOWARD! HE/HIM.
HI!
SO DO YOU LIKE TO WRITE? DRAW? **BOTH?!**

ACTUALLY, I REALLY JUST LIKE TO . . .
MAKE STUFF.
LIKE WHAT?
"COOKIES! BROWNIES!"
"SCIENTIFIC EXPERIMENTS AND MODELS!"
"NOISES! SOUNDS!"
I THOUGHT IT MIGHT BE FUN TO TRY MAKING COMICS, TOO.

MS. FATIMA GAVE US SOME COPY PAPER TO DRAW ON. IT HAS STUFF PRINTED ON ONE SIDE, SO WE'RE GIVING IT A SECOND LIFE.
I LIKE PAPER!
I'VE GOT MY FAVORITE GEL PEN! I CALL HER SUSAN.
AWW. I LIKE GEL PENS!
PENS AND PAPER. GOOD START!
UM, I ALSO BROUGHT A FEW TOOLS WITH ME.
IF THAT'S ALL RIGHT . . .

WHOA!!

THERE'S, LIKE, A WHOLE ARTS AND CRAFTS STORE IN HERE!
IT JUST KEEPS GOING!
FEEL FREE TO BORROW ANYTHING!

REGULAR PENCIL
MECHANICAL PENCIL
PAINT SET
COLORED PENCILS
SCISSORS
MODELING CLAY
STICKERS
HOLE PUNCH
ERASERS
MULTICOLOR PEN
TAPE
CRAYONS
MEASURING STUFF
GLUE
MARKERS
GEL PENS
BALLPOINT PENS
BIG MARKER
FELT-TIP PENS
SO MANY CHOICES!
BUT WHICH TOOLS ARE THE RIGHT ONES TO MAKE **COMICS** WITH?
BLACK CHARCOAL
THAT GREASY STUFF WITH A FRENCH NAME
GLUE STICK
TACKS AND PINS

AS PROMISED, I'VE BEEN RESEARCHING, AND I'M READY TO SHARE WHAT I'VE LEARNED!
OOOOOH!
Read
ALL ARE WELCOME HERE

GREAT! SO WHAT'S THE RIGHT KIND OF PEN?
AND WHICH COMES FIRST, PICTURES OR WORDS?
AND WHAT SIZE SHOULD PAGES BE?
WELL, AS I SUSPECTED, THE ANSWER TO **ALL THREE** OF THOSE QUESTIONS IS . . .
THERE **ARE** NO ANSWERS!
HUH?
COOL!!

YOU SEE, **COMICS** IS REALLY JUST A SIMPLE IDEA . . .
POP
OF PUTTING ONE PICTURE . . .
AFTER ANOTHER!

USUALLY MIXED WITH **WORDS** . . .
AND USUALLY TO TELL A **STORY**, ALTHOUGH COMICS CAN BE USED FOR OTHER THINGS.
1 2 3 4 5 6 7 8 9
AND SO COMIC STRIPS, COMIC BOOKS, MANGA, COMICS ON PHONES AND COMPUTERS, AND GRAPHIC NOVELS ARE ALL JUST . . .
COMICS!
GRRR
Smile

THE **KINDS** OF COMICS YOU CREATE OUT OF THAT SIMPLE IDEA, PICTURES IN SEQUENCE, IS UP TO YOU!
THERE ISN'T JUST ONE "RIGHT" WAY TO DO IT!
BUT ISN'T THERE SOME KIND OF SPECIAL PEN THAT THEY USE TO MAKE, Y'KNOW . . . **REAL** COMICS?
YEAH! WHAT DO THE **PROS** USE?
WELL, A FRIEND OF MINE IS A PROFESSIONAL CARTOONIST, AND SHE USES SABLE BRUSHES AND NIB PENS THAT SHE DIPS INTO INDIA INK.

OTHERS DRAW DIRECTLY ONTO COMPUTER SCREENS AND TABLETS WITH A STYLUS USING ART APPS.
BUT THERE'S NO ONE TOOL YOU HAVE TO USE AND NO ONE STYLE YOU HAVE TO WORK IN!
WOW!
THAT'S COOL TO KNOW!
SO THE ANSWER IS "SABLE BRUSH."
I WANT TO KNOW MORE ABOUT THOSE SPECIAL SCREENS AND APPS.
WAIT, SO . . .

TOSS
IF WE CAN MAKE COMICS USING **ANY** KIND OF TOOL . . .
COULD I MAKE COMICS BY PAINTING THEM ON A WALL?
SURE!
OR USING PHOTOS I TOOK?
WHY NOT?
OR WITH PAPER CUTOUTS?
OOH, YES.
OR LITTLE SCULPTURES IN BOXES?
GO FOR IT!

JUST REMEMBER THE GOLDEN RULE OF MAKING COMICS . . .
YES?
THERE **ARE** NO RULES!!
YAY!
AW, C'MON.
YAY?
LET ME KNOW IF YOU NEED ANYTHING.
WELL, THIS IS ALREADY FUN.
DO YOU HAVE ANY SABLE BRUSHES IN HERE, ART?
OH, THAT MIGHT BE THE ONE THING I **DON'T** HAVE . . .

Read!
EXCUSE ME... MAKAYLA?
I HAVE THIS.
IF YOU WANT TO BORROW IT.
IS THIS A SABLE BRUSH?!
THE KIND MS. FATIMA SAID **REAL** CARTOONISTS USE??
nod

WOW, THANKS! YOU'RE LYNDA, RIGHT?
UH-HUH.
ART, WOULD IT BE OKAY IF I BORROW THIS ERASER?
SURE!
THANK YOU.
SORRY TO BOTHER YOU!

HUH.
I GUESS SHE'S JUST SHY.

EXCUSE ME, SORRY . . .
EEP!
YOU KNOW, YOU'RE WELCOME TO JOIN US OVER THERE! WE'D LOVE TO HAVE YOU.
PLENTY OF ROOM . . . COOL TOOLS . . .
. . .
I DON'T KNOW . . .

CAN I SEE, AT LEAST?
IT'S JUST . . . I'M NOT VERY GOOD.
IT'S OKAY! WE'RE ALL HERE TO PRACTICE AND HAVE FUN.
OKAY. BUT YOU HAVE TO PROMISE NOT TO LAUGH.
CARTOONISTS CLUB PROMISE!

open
GASP!!!
IT'S TERRIBLE. I KNOW. YOU HATE IT.
LYNDA!!

ARE YOU KIDDING ME?! THIS IS BEAUTIFUL!
WAIT, REALLY?
I MEAN, YOUR PEOPLE... THEY LOOK LIKE PEOPLE!
AND YOU HAVE ALL THESE DIFFERENT POSES...

AND ACTIONS THAT TELL A STORY ...
Smash
(Bump)
AND FACES THAT SHOW FEELINGS!

YOU'RE SO NICE, BUT . . .
WHEN I LOOK AT THEM, ALL I SEE ARE MY MISTAKES.
I WISH I COULD MAKE "MISTAKES" THIS GOOD.
COME ON -- YOU DON'T HAVE TO SHOW OFF YOUR WORK, BUT LET US SHOW YOU OURS.
OKAY.
HAT MAN!
Ha Ha
GASP
HOWARD, YOU'RE SO FUNNY . . . SO CREATIVE . . .

YOU'RE MUCH BRAVER THAN I AM.
YOU DRAW ANYTHING YOU WANT ...
EVEN WHEN YOU HAVE NO IDEA **HOW** TO DRAW IT!
Ha Ha
OH NO. THAT SOUNDED SO MEAN ...
BUT SOOOO TRUE!!!
Ha Ha Ha Ha Ha Ha Ha Ha Ha Ha Ha
MISTAKES ARE COOL. THEY'RE HOW WE LEARN.
YEAH. I MADE THE MISTAKE OF USING A CUP OF **SALT** INSTEAD OF SUGAR IN MY FIRST BATCH OF BROWNIES ...
AND WHEN MY PARENTS ATE THEM, I LEARNED THAT THEY CAN MAKE SOME REALLY FUNNY **FACES.**

TIME TO CLOSE UP! HOW DID YOUR FIRST MEETING GO?
GREAT!
LYNDA IS HELPING US ALL DRAW BETTER!
WE HAVE OUR FIRST COVER!
AND I MADE A DINOSAUR COMIC OUT OF JUICE BOXES!
EVIL NUGGET VS. TOFU-PUP

EXCELLENT!
DID YOU HAVE FUN, LYNDA?
Read
nod
DOES THIS MEAN YOU'D LIKE TO JOIN THE CLUB?
YES.
YAAAAY!
WOO-HOO!

CHAPTER FOUR

HOWARD? LIGHTS OUT.
KNOCK KNOCK
JUST FIVE MORE MINUTES, DAD . . .
I'M STUDYING!
THE BIG BOOK OF DOG GUY
COMMON CORE
FULL COLOR DOG GUY
#1 BESTSELLER DOG GUY PAWS UP
HELP!
WILL NO ONE SAVE ME?
!
BUT I'M STILL TIED UP!
OH. GOOD POINT.
CHUG CHUG
DOG GUY IS HERE!

GOOD!
?
giggle!
KNOCK KNOCK!
SOMETHING FUNNY IN YOUR MATH TEXTBOOK?

SORRY, DAD.
WHAT DID WE PROMISE?
"NO COMICS ON SCHOOL NIGHTS."
click
BBQ
ZZZ

... AND THEN TOFU PUP ASKS MR. NUGGET ...
"Y ARE YOU SO EVIL?"
HI, HOWARD! HI, MAKAYLA!
HA HA HA!
ALL ARE WELCOME HERE
OH, ARE WE LATE TO TODAY'S MEETING?
NO, WE JUST GOT HERE EARLY.
WE'RE READING BATTLE PRINCESS KISHIMOTO.
IT'S **SO** GOOD.

OKAY, CLUB ... READY TO MAKE SOME **TERRIBLE COMICS??**
YEEEEA-
WAIT, WHAT?
I THOUGHT WE WERE GONNA LEARN HOW TO MAKE **GOOD** COMICS!
YEAH.
YOU'VE GOT TO START SOMEWHERE.

WHEN I WAS IN MIDDLE SCHOOL, MY FRIENDS AND I PLAYED A COMICS-MAKING GAME CALLED QUANTO COMICS.
YOU START WITH AN ORDINARY PIECE OF PAPER...
THEN YOU MAKE A TITLE LOGO ON TOP.
I'LL GIVE YOU FIVE MINUTES.
WHAT KIND OF TITLE?
ANYTHING AT ALL! JUST NOT TOO SPECIFIC.
SO, NOT "ALBERT EINSTEIN AND BEYONCÉ GO TO SAN DIEGO TO BUY MY AUNT LULU A NEW VACUUM CLEANER FROM THE APPLIANCE STORE NEXT TO THE FROZEN YOGURT PLACE"?

YES. THAT WOULD BE TOO SPECIFIC.
OH! AND NOT TOO GENERAL, EITHER.
SO NOT, LIKE . . .
"STUFF."
EXACTLY.
AAAAND . . . GO!
TAP
EEK!
KIKI'S BAD HAIR DAY
ROBOT VERSUS COWBOY
Best in Show
DINOSAUR DANCE PARTY

EXCELLENT! **GREAT** LOGOS.
NOW WE DRAW?
GET YOUR PENS AND PENCILS READY, AAAAAND ...
HAND YOUR PAPER TO THE PERSON ON YOUR **LEFT!**
WHAT--
OH!
HA HA
NICE.
OR ACROSS THE TABLE, IN ART'S CASE.
OOH, COLORS. AND DRAWING DINOSAURS COULD BE FUN.
THANKS, ART!
WOW, EVEN LYNDA'S **TITLES** ARE PRETTY.

BAD HAIR DAY... OH, THAT'S GREAT, MAKAYLA!
WOW, I LOVE DRAWING ROBOTS, HOWARD!
BUT WHAT'S A COWDOY?
HUH?
SHOULD BE COWB-- OH, WHOOPS!
I'LL FIX IT.
scribble scribble
AH...
COWDOG IT IS!
YOU HAVE TWENTY MINUTES TO DRAW YOUR COMICS...
EEP!
STARTING NOW!

-TICK- TICK -TICK -TICK -TICK-
DRAW DRAW DRAW DRAW DRAW
ding!
TIME'S UP! LET'S SEE YOUR COMICS.
Best in Show
Be happy, Pierre! you are Best in Show!
But how can I be Happy when so many dogs are suffering?
Show Dogs of the world UNITE!!
(to help OTHER dogs.)
Greetings Sad Mixed Breed dog! we are here to save you.
?
But I am not sad! I am loved by my owner Makayla even though I am smelly and bark too much.
Also U.R. Patronizing
the END...
(...for Patronizing Show Dogs)
I USED LYNDA'S TITLE FOR A SILLY DOG COMIC!

KiKi's BAD HAIR DAY
Brush Brush
OH, KiKi! YOUR HAIR IS SO GOOD!
NO, MY HAIR IS BAD.
oh no not again
RRAR!!
BAD HAIR! STOP IT!
I WILL DEFEAT BAD HAIR!
My Hero!
Shampoo Man
WAIT, I AM ALSO A SUPERHERO!
AND ME!
Condi-tioner
ME TOO!
AAH! I AM TOILET PAPER!!
HA! YOU THINK YOUR COMIC IS SILLY . . .
LOOK WHAT I DID WITH YOUR TITLE!
THESE ARE BOTH SO GREAT . . .
HA HA HA HA HA HA
I LOVE THE TOILET PAPER! SO RANDOM!

LOGO BY HOWARD
COMIC BY ART!
ROBOT VERSUS Cowdog
"Cowdog" INVENTED BY HOWARD
HERE'S THE ONE I DID FROM HOWARD'S TITLE!
I ARREST YOU, COWDOG IN THE NAME OF ROBOT LAW!
I arrest you Robot in the name of COWDOG LAW!
But who is RIGHT ?
I USED SOME ANIMAL STICKERS!
Uh-Oh! They both have Sherrif Stars. Also nobody broke a law anyway.
COURTHOUSE
You must stop fighting and be friends and get ice cream.
JUDGE GAVEL FACE
BUT I AM A ROBOT AND HAVE NO STOMACH.
And I am Lactose Intolerant!!
(Sniff) I am a terrible judge.
NO JUDGE YOU'RE RIGHT. WE HAVE A THING IN COMMON NOW AND ARE FRIENDS.
They have nothing in common really.
Hee Hee!
COWDOG IS REAL! BE STILL MY HEART!
CAN WE SEE **YOURS,** LYNDA?

DINOSAUR
DANCE PARTY
Everybody Dance!
I COULDN'T EVEN FINISH THE FIRST PANEL.
?

!!
SO BEAUTIFUL.
THAT IS A PERFECT T. REX HEAD.
I WANTED TO DO A **WHOLE** COMIC, BUT I WASTED ALL MY TIME GETTING THE HEAD RIGHT!
IT WASN'T A WASTE. THE REST OF US WERE JUST A LITTLE... MESSIER.
THESE ARE CALLED QUANTO COMICS BECAUSE THEY'RE ALL ABOUT THE QUANTITY, **NOT** THE QUALITY!
SO YOU MAKE A **LOT** OF MESSY DRAWINGS INSTEAD OF ONE PERFECT DRAWING?
YEAH!

MS. FATIMA, MAY I HAVE ANOTHER FIFTEEN MINUTES?
OF COURSE!
WILL YOU HELP ME BE MESSY??
WE'D LOVE TO!
CARTOONISTS CLUB **TEAM EFFORT!**
WOO!
THAT'S IT, JUST ADD A BODY.
IT'S OKAY IF IT'S TOO SMALL, IT'S FUNNIER THAT WAY.
ADD SOME SPIKES!
AND SOUND EFFECTS!
I HAVE MORE STICKERS!
OH! YOU COULD ADD MUSICAL NOTES!
MAYBE GLITTER?
YEAH!
OR IS THAT **TOO** MESSY? . . .
HA HA!

DINOSAUR
DANCE PARTY
Everybody Dance!
Rumble
Rumble
Ding! Dong!
Who is at the Door?
It is A Meteor!
I Bring Cola.
NO METEORS ALLOWED!
DINOS FOREVER
THE END

NOW THAT'S A MESS.
A **BEAUTIFUL** MESS!
BZZZ

OOH, MY DAD WILL BE HERE SOON! HE WANTS TO KNOW, DOES ANYBODY NEED A RIDE HOME?
I WANNA MEET YOUR DAD!
IF YOU'RE GOING, I WANNA GO!
ASK YOUR PARENTS IF IT'S OKAY!
Text Text Text
...LYNDA?
THANKS, ART. MAYBE ANOTHER TIME.

AND SO:
CRAFT MIDDLE SCHOOL
BLAH BLAH BLAH BLAH BLAH STORIES HUMOR COMICS BOOKS READING WRITING DRAWING BLAH BLAH BLAH BLAH BLAH BLAH BLAH BLAH BLAH BLAH BLAH BLAH BLAH . . .

...AND WE CALL THEM QUANTO COMICS!
COOL!
MY FRIENDS AND I DID STUFF LIKE THAT IN MIDDLE SCHOOL, TOO.
THOSE WERE HAPPY MEMORIES.
I **MISS** THOSE DAYS.

SO IS THE CLUB GOING TO MAKE ZINES?
WHAT'S A ZINE?
WELL, THE NAME IS KINDA LIKE A SHORT VERSION OF "MAGAZINE"...
. . .
DO YOU KNOW WHAT MAGAZINES ARE?
THEY HAVE SOME OLD ONES AT THE LIBRARY!

ART, REACH INTO MY BACKPACK...
I HAVE SOME ZINES THAT I BOUGHT AT A COMICS SHOP LAST WEEK.
DISTRACTIBLE FROG COMIX
50¢
COOL! THESE LOOK HANDMADE!
THEY ARE!
PIRATE CAT
LOST in Boston

WHO MAKES THESE?
ZINES AND MINICOMICS ARE USUALLY PRINTED, FOLDED, AND STAPLED BY THE CREATORS THEMSELVES!
See you Tomorrow!
IN FACT, YOU CAN MAKE ONE FROM A **SINGLE SHEET OF PAPER!**
WHAAAAT?
SHOCKED COMICS

I CAN TEACH YOU TONIGHT, ART!
OKAY!
ART, YOU **HAVE TO SHOW US HOW** AT OUR NEXT MEETING!
OKAY!!

CHAPTER FIVE

ALL ARE WELCOME HERE
TAP TAP TAP TAP TAP TAP
I WISH ART WOULD HURRY UP AND GET HERE ...
I CAN'T WAIT TO LEARN ABOUT MINICOMICS!
TAP TAP TAP TAP TAP TAP TAP
TAP TAP TAP TA T
TAP TAP TAP

TAP TAP TAP

Sketch Sketch
Sketch Sketch
...
TAP
TAP TAP
TAP...
...
My Mami and Papi used to love to dance.
Papi was going to teach me how!
But then...

Sniff
OH MY GOSH -- ARE YOU OKAY?
UM ... IT'S JUST ... THE TAPPING PEN BROUGHT UP A MEMORY.
I'M SORRY. I'LL TRY NOT TO DO IT AGAIN.
NO, IT'S OKAY.
IT WAS A MEMORY WORTH WRITING DOWN.

LIBRARY
HOW'S YOUR BIG INTERGALACTIC SERIES GOING, MAKAYLA?
EPICALLY.
I'VE DECIDED THAT PRINCESS HIKARU'S HOME WORLD HAS SEVEN MOONS . . .
AND ON EACH MOON IS A SHARD OF FLAMING SCEPTER GUARDED BY WINGED TIGERS . . .
I'VE BEEN DESIGNING ALL THESE COOL COSTUMES FOR THE ROYAL FAMILY . . .

SOUNDS AMAZING!
CAN WE SEE SOME PAGES?
UM...
I HAVEN'T ACTUALLY DRAWN ANY YET. OR, YOU KNOW, WRITTEN THEM.
WE ARE GOING TO CHANGE THAT TODAY!!!
I'M HERE!! ARE WE STILL MAKING MINICOMICS TODAY?
YEP! ARE YOU READY?

OKAY, ART ... TAKE IT AWAY!
AHEM.
SO, FIRST OF ALL, MY DAD TOLD ME THESE THINGS HAVE ALL DIFFERENT SORTS OF NAMES.
• ZINES
• ASHCANS
• MINICOMICS
AND THEY ALL FIT INTO THE OVERALL TERM "SELF-PUBLISHED COMICS."
EVERYONE HAVE A PIECE OF BLANK PAPER? GOOD!

NOW, LET'S FOLD THE PAPER INTO QUARTERS.
1.
"FIRST, LENGTH-WISE."
2.
"THEN, WIDTH-WISE."
SO, RIGHT AWAY, YOU HAVE A TINY EIGHT-PAGE BOOKLET ...
flip flip
BUT WITH SOME PAGES STILL ATTACHED HERE AT THE TOP WHERE IT FOLDS.
3.
"NOW, WITH JUST A LIGHT PENCIL LINE, MARK THE FRONT AND BACK COVERS."
FRONT COVER
BACK COVE

4.
"THEN, MARK THE PAGE NUMBERS, TOO. MAYBE UNDERLINE THEM SO IT'S EASY TO TELL WHICH WAY IS UP."
SNEAK YOUR PENCIL INSIDE THE FOLD-Y BITS.
5.
NOW, UNFOLD . . .
SO **SIDE A** LOOKS LIKE THIS . . .
AND **SIDE B** LOOKS LIKE THIS.
6.
BACK COVER
FRONT COVER
7.
NOW, DRAW YOUR COMICS PAGES TO MATCH THE ORDER.
ANY KIND OF COMIC YOU WANT!
FOUR!
THREE!
...AND THAT'S...
THE END
FRONT COVER COMICS
TWO!
FIVE!
ONE!
SIX!

NOW, YOU **COULD** JUST FOLD IT BACK UP AND STAPLE AND TRIM IT FOR YOUR VERY OWN, ONE-OF-A-KIND, **SINGLE** MINICOMIC . . .
BUT **TODAY** . . .
WE'LL TAKE THAT TWO-SIDED SHEET OF COMIC ART . . .
FOUR!
THREE!
...AND THAT'S...
THE END
FRONT COVER COMICS
8.
AND USE EITHER A SCANNER AND A PRINTER . . .
OR AN OLD-FASHIONED PHOTOCOPIER . . .
TO MAKE TWO-SIDED **COPIES.**
VRRR
KA-CHUNK
VRRR
KA-CHUNK
9.
"THAT WAY, YOU CAN STAPLE . . ."
FRONT COVER COMICS
CHONK!
10.
"AND TRIM THE FOLD-Y BITS OFF TO MAKE . . ."
snip!
FRONT COVER COMICS
11.
"AS MANY COPIES OF YOUR MINICOMIC AS YOU WANT!"
FRONT COVER COMICS

SO ... ONLY SIX PAGES?
WELL, EIGHT IF YOU COUNT THE COVERS.
Read!
BUT I CAN'T TELL A STORY IN ONLY SIX PAGES!
HIKARU'S BACKSTORY **ALONE** IS GOING TO TAKE 200 PAGES!!
SO START SMALL.

LIKE, WHAT DOES HIKARU HAVE FOR BREAKFAST?
PANCAKES?
MAKE SIX PAGES ABOUT THAT.
WHAT DOES SHE SEE WALKING TO SCHOOL IN THE MORNING?
CATS ... AN ICE CREAM TRUCK ...
A STRANGE GLOW DESCENDING FROM THE CLOUDS ...?
MAKE SIX PAGES ABOUT **THAT!**
BUT WHY WOULD ANYONE WANT TO READ IT?!
I'D READ THAT ...
ME TOO.
IT SOUNDS INTERESTING!

SMALL COMICS ARE A GREAT WAY TO SHARE SMALL MOMENTS ...
OR SET UP A FUNNY PUNCH LINE ...
OR JUST LET THE READER INTO YOUR WORLD FOR A LITTLE WHILE.
HMM ...

OKAY, SO, LIKE, HIKARU IS WALKING TO SCHOOL.
RIGHT, WHERE YOU MARKED "1" IN PENCIL ON YOUR FOLDED PAGE.
OH NO, I DREW HER FOOT ALL WEIRD!

ERASER?
THANKS.
erase erase
erase erase
OKAY... NOW WHAT?
NOW YOU MAKE UP THE REST OF THE STORY.
...
.....
....

AAAAAUGH! THIS IS TOO HARD!!
crunch
crumple
BUT, MAKAYLA . . .
YOU HAVE MORE IDEAS THAN ANY OF US!
BUT WHICH ONES DO I PICK? WHICH DO I LEAVE OUT?
WHAT MAKES A STORY A **STORY?**

PERSONALLY, I FIND IT EASIER TO START STORIES WHEN I KNOW WHAT MY CHARACTERS WANT.
Read!
AFTER ALL, THERE AREN'T MANY STORIES THAT GO ALL THE WAY FROM A CHARACTER'S BIRTH TO THEIR DEATH ...
BUT THERE ARE LOTS OF STORIES THAT START WHEN A CHARACTER STARTS WANTING SOMETHING ...
AND END WHEN THEY GET IT, OR THEY DON'T.
OR MAYBE **CHANGE** WHAT THEY WANT!

SO WHAT DOES HIKARU WANT, MAKAYLA?
WELL, TO FIND THE GEMSTONE AND ALL THE PIECES OF THE FLAMING SWORD AND TO UNITE HER HOME WORLD AND BRING JUSTICE TO THE UNIVERSE AND TO FIND A GROUP OF BEST FRIENDS . . .
ALL WHILE WALKING TO SCHOOL?
OH.
RIGHT.

WHEN YOU'RE MAKING A **BIG** STORY, A CHARACTER MIGHT WANT **BIG** THINGS.
ead!
BUT FOR A **SMALL** STORY, MAYBE THEY WANT SOMETHING A BIT . . . SMALLER?
CAN I MAKE A SUGGESTION, MAKAYLA?
SURE.
WHAT IF HIKARU HAS THE GEMSTONE ALREADY BUT HASN'T UNLOCKED ITS POWER YET . . .
BUT AS SHE PASSES BY THE ICE CREAM TRUCK, THE SKY STARTS GLOWING BECAUSE HER POWER IS GROWING . . .
YEAH . . .
OH! AND THE GEMSTONE IS GLOWING, TOO!
AND GETTING WARMER!

MAYBE IT'S HUMMING, TOO.
YEAH! THEN THE ICE CREAM TRUCK DRIVER SAYS "HI" ...
WHICH **DISTRACTS** HIKARU JUST LONG ENOUGH ...
...
OH! OH! FOR ONE OF THE CATS TO **LEAP** OUT ...
AND **SNATCH** THE GEMSTONE WITH ITS **TEETH!**
YEAH!!
AND THEN THE CAT RUNS WITH IT ACROSS THE STREET!!
WITH HIKARU CHASING RIGHT BEHIND!
HA HA!
NO RUNNING IN THE LIBRARY!

WAIT!
WE CAN'T USE OUR AWESOME IDEA.
WHY NOT??
MS. FATIMA SAID BIG STORIES INCLUDE CHARACTERS WANTING **BIG** THINGS . . .
AND LITTLE STORIES INCLUDE CHARACTERS WANTING **LITTLE** THINGS . . .
?
BUT TO MY CHARACTER, THE GEMSTONE ISN'T A LITTLE THING AT ALL.
IT'S **EVERYTHING!**

DON'T WORRY, MAKAYLA. IF YOU HAVE A STORY YOU LIKE, GO FOR IT! THE BIG/LITTLE THING ISN'T A RULE OR ANYTHING.
BESIDES, "LITTLE" DOESN'T HAVE TO MEAN **UNIMPORTANT.**
YOUR READERS JUST NEED TO KNOW THAT IT'S IMPORTANT TO HIKARU!
TAP TAP TAP TAP TAP
HMMMMM.
sketch sketch sketch

FINISHED!!!!!!!
OOH, CAN I READ IT?
ME TOO!
ME THREE!
NO. NOT UNTIL IT'S PUBLISHED.
TO THE PHOTOCOPIER!!!

ZOOOM
HOW'S IT GOING, LYNDA?
STILL SLOW.
I'VE ONLY PENCILED THREE AND A HALF PAGES.
HEY, THEY'RE GOOD PAGES!
I'M DOING THIS SILLY STORY ABOUT THE MOON ... I'VE DRAWN AND ERASED IT A MILLION TIMES.
(Back Cover)

I CAN'T ALWAYS JUST WRITE "DANCE PARTY!" AT THE TOP OF A PAGE.
IF SOMETHING IS REALLY STUMPING YOU -- THE STORY OR THE ART -- IT'S OKAY TO SKIP OVER THAT PART AND COME BACK TO IT LATER.
?
BUT... EVERYONE ELSE IS FINISHED! HOW CAN I EVER BE A **REAL** CARTOONIST IF I CAN'T EVEN FINISH A SIX-PAGE MINICOMIC?
AND WHAT IF **WRITER-ME** DECIDES TO CHANGE WHAT'S IN A PANEL...
AFTER **ARTIST-ME** HAS ALREADY DRAWN IT?
A
B C
HOW DO I **PLAN?**

HAVE YOU HEARD OF **THUMBNAILS?**
IS THAT LIKE A FINGERNAIL?
IT'S A TERM FOR . . . A **ROUGH DRAFT.** A **SKETCH.** KIND OF LIKE STORYBOARDS.
CARTOONISTS OFTEN "THUMBNAIL" THEIR PAGES BEFORE CREATING THEIR FINISHED ARTWORK, SO THEY CAN "READ" THEIR COMICS IN DRAFT FORM.
HERE'S WHAT THE PREVIOUS TWO PAGES MIGHT LOOK LIKE AS THUMBNAILS.
HUH!
HOW'S IT GOING, LYNDA?
STILL SLOW...
I'VE ONLY DRAWN THREE AND A HALF PAGES.
HEY, THEY'RE GOOD PAGES!
TOP OF A PAGE.
OKAY TO SKIP THAT PART COME BACK IT LATER.
BUT... EVERYONE ELSE IS FINISHED! HOW CAN I EVER BE A REAL CARTOONIST IF I CAN'T EVEN FINISH A 6-PAGE MINICOMIC??
AND WHAT IF WRITER-ME DECIDES TO CHANGE WHAT'S IN A PANEL—
—AFTER ARTIST-ME HAS ALREADY DRAWN IT?
HOW DO I PLAN?

I CAN DO STICK FIGURES FOR NOW?
SURE! AND NOW YOU HAVE A BLUEPRINT -- A **TEMPLATE** -- FOR YOUR FINISHED COMIC!
YOU CAN DRAW THE FINAL ART AT HOME, AND WE'LL PHOTOCOPY IT NEXT TIME!
I CAN'T WAIT!
MEANWHILE . . .
UGH, IT'S WRONG AGAIN!
OH NO! UPSIDE DOWN IS RIGHT SIDE UP IS --
I CAN DO IT.

Beep
Beep
Boop
Ger-SHLUNK
Ger-SHLUNK
shhhh-LIFF
IT'S A MATCH.
PLEASE LET THIS WORK... PLEASE LET THIS WORK...
ALL ARE WELCOME HERE

OKAY. FOLD ONCE...
LINE UP THE CORNERS.
SHE KNOWS.
YEAH, FLATTEN THE --
SHE KNOWS!
AND... FOLD... AGAIN.
AAAAAAAND...
READY?
READY!

STAPLER.
GULP
WON'T REACH!
HERE, TRY CURLING IT OVER JUST A BIT . . .
YEAH. THANKS.
K-CHNK
K-CHNK

SCISSORS.
trimmm trimmm
YOU DID IT!
THERE'S SOMETHING **NEW** IN THE WORLD BECAUSE OF YOU.
HIKARU VERSUS the Cat!
By Makay

YOU! RANDOM LIBRARY KID VOLUNTEER! WANNA BUY MY COMIC?
MY NAME IS JEFF, MAKAYLA.
GRAPHIC NOVELS
I LITERALLY SIT BEHIND YOU IN HOMEROOM.
. . .
JEFF, PLEASE BUY MY COMIC!
SURE, HOW MUCH?
UH. FIFTY CENTS?
OKAY.
HEY, THIS IS PRETTY GOOD!

I'M A COMICS PRO!!!!!

WOOOOOOOOOO
HOOOOOOOOOOO!!

CHAPTER SIX

TWO WEEKS LATER
NOW, CLASS . . .
YOU ALL REMEMBER THE DIFFERENCE BETWEEN CONSTANTS AND VARIABLES, RIGHT? ANYONE?
ANYONE BESIDES KAZU?
KNOW THE CODE

"VARIABLE" IS THE PART WE DON'T KNOW YET?
YES, MAKAYLA. CLOSE ENOUGH.
THE "VARIABLE" REFERS TO THE UNKNOWN IN A PROBLEM...
PSST...
...DEPENDING ON THE CONTEXT, AND WE TEND TO USE SYMBOLS SUCH AS "X" OR "Y" TO REPRESENT...
HA HA!
SO THEY DEPEND ON CONTEXT.
CAN I HAVE ONE?
HOWARD, CAREFUL...

WHAT'S THAT?
CAN I SEE?
ME TOO!
Heh
hee hee!
YOU'RE **SO** GONNA GET IN TROUBLE AGAIN . . .
CONSTANTS, ON THE OTHER HAND,
PASS 'EM DOWN!
ARE A KNOWN . . .
SO THE CONSTANT . . .
IS, UH, THE SAME IN . . .
UH . . .
21
5
3
8
13
GUFFAW!
SNRK!
HEE!
GIGGLE!
HA HA!

WHAT IS SO FUNNY???
HAHAHA HA
HA HA
HA HA HA HA
HA HA HA
HA HA HA HA

I'LL BE BACK IN A MOMENT, CLASS. PLEASE STUDY THE CHART ON PAGE 37.
102
HOWARD . . .
THIS IS . . .
flip
102
ACTUALLY, THIS IS PRETTY GOOD!
!

HEH!
TOFU PUP REMINDS ME OF MY CHILDHOOD DOG, EUCLID.
AND I'M IMPRESSED YOU MADE IT INTO THIS LITTLE BOOKLET ...
MINICOMIC!
10
WAIT, SO ...
YOU'RE NOT MAD?
WELL, YOUR MATH SCORES ARE FINE, BUT THE CONSTANT DISRUPTIONS TO MY CLASS ARE CONCERNING.
102

I MIGHT NEED TO ARRANGE A CONFERENCE WITH YOUR PARENTS TO DISCUSS --
NO!!
PLEASE, MR. RUGGETT... MY DAD HATES COMICS!!
DOES HE KNOW YOU'RE A CARTOONIST?

RING!
HOWARD, WAIT UP!
WHAT DID HE SAY?
114
IS HE GOING TO TALK TO YOUR DAD?
WILL YOU GET IN TROUBLE?
YEAH, PROBABLY ...

SO WHY DON'T YOU LOOK MORE UPSET?!
MAKAYLA, MR. R. CALLED ME A "CARTOONIST," AND ... AND ... I THINK HE'S RIGHT!
I THINK **I AM** A CARTOONIST!
WELL, DUH ... YOU'RE IN THE CARTOONISTS CLUB!
I MEAN FOR **REAL!**
I THINK IT MIGHT BE **WHO I AM** ... WHO I WANT TO BE!
WOW. THAT'S GREAT, THEN ... CONGRATULATIONS!

choco moo
HOWARD'S DECIDED HE'S A CARTOONIST FOR REAL!
COOL! I DECIDED I'M AN ANTHROPOLOGIST, BUT I KEEP CHANGING MY MIND.
I WANT TO DRAW STUFF AS A JOB SOMEDAY.
YOU'RE SO GOOD! I BET YOU CAN DO IT.

I WANT TO BE A MULTIMEDIA STORYTELLER.
I'LL START IN COMICS WITH MY TWELVE-VOLUME EPIC ...
THEN I'LL WRITE AND DIRECT THE MOVIE ADAPTATION ...
AND THE SPIN-OFF TV SERIES ...
I WANT PEOPLE TO KNOW MY NAME.
HA! I THINK EVERYONE IN SCHOOL KNOWS YOUR NAME.
NO, BUT LIKE -- I WANT THEM TO KNOW ME FOR THE THINGS I CREATE!
IS IT WRONG TO WANT MY VOICE TO BE HEARD?
EXCUSE ME.
NO, BUT --

OH, HI, JEFF-FROM-HOMEROOM.
HI, MAKAYLA. IS ISSUE NUMBER THREE OUT YET?
YEP. GOT IT RIGHT HERE. NEW ISSUE EVERY WEEK!
COULD WE BUY THREE COPIES, PLEASE?
"WE"?
OH, SORRY -- THIS IS TRINA AND CECE!
I REALLY LIKED ISSUE NUMBER TWO. I CAN'T WAIT TO SEE WHAT HAPPENS NEXT.
YOU ARE SO CREATIVE.
COOL! THANK YOU FOR READING.
OOH, NICE COVER.
CAN I SHAKE YOUR HAND?

OH. UH.
SURE!
TH-THANK YOU!
BYE, MAKAYLA! LOOKING FORWARD TO ISSUE NUMBER FOUR.
NICE MEETING YOU.
EEEEE!
YOU WERE SAYING? . . .

RINNNNNNG!!
CRAFT MIDDLE SCH
LIBRARY
TAP
TAP
TAP
TAP
TAP
TAP
TAP
ARE

STILL WORKING ON YOUR BIG COLOR COMIC, LYNDA?
UM . . .
I AM. BUT I DON'T KNOW IF I WANT ANYONE TO SEE IT JUST YET.
STILL FEELING UNSURE ABOUT YOUR ARTWORK?
ACTUALLY . . .
I **LIKE** THE ART. I LIKE THE STORY, TOO. IT'S JUST . . .
IT'S REALLY PERSONAL.

IT WOULD FEEL LIKE PEOPLE WERE READING MY DIARY!
YOU KNOW . . .
MEMOIR IS A VERY POPULAR GENRE OF COMICS!
WHAT'S MEMOIR? AND WHAT'S A **GENRE?**
GENRE MEANS A CATEGORY OF SUBJECT MATTER.
?
JUST LIKE MOVIES, BOOKS, AND VIDEOS CAN BE ABOUT ANY SUBJECT -- COMICS CAN BE, TOO!
• ACTION COMICS
• HUMOR COMICS
• ROMANCE COMICS
• FANTASY COMICS
• PRETTY MUCH ANYTHING YOU CAN THINK OF
(COMICS THEMSELVES AREN'T A GENRE. THEY'RE A FORM OF STORYTELLING THAT CAN CONTAIN MANY GENRES!)

MEMOIR IS BASED ON THE LATIN WORD FOR **MEMORY.**
SOME CARTOONISTS MAKE JOURNAL COMICS EVERY DAY.
On Monday, I went whale watching with Grandpa...
LOOK!
AYE, THAR SHE BLOWS!
03 | MONDAY JULY
WHY CANT YOU TAKE THE TRASH OUT?
BIP! BIP!
MUST! FIGHT! MONSTER
CLIK! CLIK!
SIS TRIED COOKING...
TASTE THIS.
MMM...
WHAT DO YOU THINK?
Gulp
IT'S... GREAT!
Monday, July 3
BELL
El Deafo
REAL FRIENDS
Smile
WHEN STARS ARE SCATTERED
CHAN
UPROOTED
Siegel Siegel
to dance
PARACHUTE
BE PREPARED
LITTLE WHITE DUCK
THE NEW
FAJARDO
Miss Quinces
FOUR EYES
timid
THE TRY
WEAVER
WEIRDO
SOME WAIT YEARS AND THEN WRITE AND ILLUSTRATE THEIR MEMORIES!

THERE ARE DIFFERENT NAMES FOR THIS: AUTOBIO, OR AUTOBIOGRAPHY. NARRATIVE NONFICTION.
OR... DIARY!
MEMOIR COMICS CAN BE **VERY** VALIDATING FOR A READER.
SOMETIMES A PERSON FEELS ALONE...
UNTIL THEY READ SOMETHING THEY CAN RELATE TO.
AND, SUDDENLY, THEY FEEL SEEN AND UNDERSTOOD!
El Deafo
CECE BELL

AS A MEMOIRIST, IT'S IMPORTANT TO DECIDE WHAT **YOU** FEEL COMFORTABLE SHARING!
AND IT'S PERFECTLY OKAY TO DECIDE NOT TO SHARE.
OR TO WAIT A WHILE.
THANK YOU, MS. FATIMA.
OF COURSE.
HOWDY!

HI, ART!
ARE YOU TWO READY WITH YOUR SECRET ASSIGNMENT?
YEP!
I HOPE SO . . .
WHAT?? NO WAY!
?
?
Read
HOW COULD HE BE YOUR FAVORITE CHARACTER? HE'S A BIG JERK!
THAT'S 'CAUSE YOU HAVEN'T READ VOLUME THIRTEEN YET!
LET ME GUESS: ARE WE TALKING ABOUT PRINCE ZURX IN *BATTLE PRINCESS KISHIMOTO* AGAIN?
YES.
ALL ARE WELCOME HERE

OOH! VOLUME THIRTEEN!!!
ALL YOURS.
I'M WITH HOWARD. I LIKE PRINCE ZURX.
HE'S A GOOD CHARACTER! YOU CAN SEE HIM CHANGE WHAT HE WANTS AND TRY TO BE A BETTER PERSON.
YOU CAN TELL HE HAS ALL THESE INNER CONFLICTS.
YEAH, EVEN WHEN HE'S NOT **SAYING** ANYTHING!
EXACTLY! AND, SPEAKING OF WHICH, I BELIEVE ART AND LYNDA HAVE SOME THOUGHTS TO SHARE ON HOW CARTOONISTS CAN **SHOW** THINGS LIKE THAT.

SO MS. FATIMA CHALLENGED LYNDA AND ME TO LEARN ABOUT HOW FACES AND BODIES SHOW FEELINGS!
MY DAD SHOWED ME SOME VIDEOS . . .
AND MS. FATIMA SHOWED ME SOME BOOKS!
AND WE LEARNED ALL ABOUT **FACIAL EXPRESSIONS AND BODY LANGUAGE!**
YOU CAN GO FIRST, ART.

AHEM
SO, WHEN YOU THINK ABOUT IT, FACES ARE LIKE THESE AMAZING MACHINES.
MACHINES?
YEAH, YOU HAVE ALL THESE MUSCLES THAT MOVE PARTS OF YOUR FACE IN DIFFERENT WAYS . . .
SOMETIMES IT'S FOR PRACTICAL STUFF LIKE OPENING YOUR MOUTH TO EAT.
BUT, MOSTLY, IT'S JUST TO SHOW THE WORLD ALL THE **EMOTIONS** YOU'RE FEELING ON THE INSIDE.
ALMOST LIKE FACES CAN SEND THOUGHTS!

AND THE BEST THING ABOUT DRAWING FACES IS THAT EVEN A SUPER **SIMPLE** DRAWING, LIKE A SMILEY FACE --
IT'S A GIANT EMOJI!
CAN TRICK YOUR BRAIN INTO **FEELING** THAT EMOTION.
AWW!
HERE ARE SIX SIMPLE FACES. CAN YOU NAME THE EMOTIONS?
EASY!

HAPPY.
SAD.
SCARED.
GROSSED OUT.
MAD.
AND, UM . . .
SURPRISED!
EXACTLY! SO ARE THOSE THE ONLY EMOTIONS? WHAT ARE SOME OTHERS?
STUFFY.
FLIRTY!
GOOFY!
AMUSED.
SNEAKY!
UM . . .
STRICT.
EMBARRASSED!
CONCENTRATING!
SYMPATHETIC!
SUSPICIOUS.
EXCITED!
CONFUSED.
STUBBORN.
RELIEVED.
GUILTY!
NERVOUS.
PROUD.
YEAH . . . HUNDREDS OF CHOICES, RIGHT?

BUT MY DAD SAYS THESE SIX EXPRESSIONS ARE **SPECIAL** ...
BECAUSE THEY'RE THE SIX THAT EVERYBODY ALL OVER THE WORLD CAN RECOGNIZE ...
JOY
SADNESS
FEAR
ANGER
SURPRISE
DISGUST
AND THEY'RE THE INGREDIENTS YOU NEED TO START DRAWING ALL THE **OTHER** EXPRESSIONS!
"INGREDIENTS"?
LIKE IN A RECIPE?
THAT'S RIGHT!

SOMETIMES YOU ONLY NEED A PINCH OF **ONE** INGREDIENT.
LIKE, JUST A PINCH OF **ANGER** CAN MAKE A FACE LOOK **STERN.**
OR JUST A PINCH OF **FEAR** CAN MAKE A FACE LOOK **NERVOUS.**
BUT A PINCH OF **ANGER** . . .
PLUS A PINCH OF **SADNESS** . . .
MAKES:
I'M VERY **DISAPPOINTED** IN YOU, HOWARD.
EEK!
OH! SO JOY PLUS ANGER WOULD BE . . . **MEAN.**
YES! WHILE JOY PLUS SURPRISE WOULD BE **DELIGHT.**
AH! AND JOY PLUS DISGUST WOULD BE THE **"EWWWW"** FACE!

IT'S LIKE WHEN YOU MIX COLORS TOGETHER IN WATERCOLORS, EXCEPT YOU'RE **MIXING FACES!**
YEP. AND, IF YOU'RE DRAWING **CARTOONY** FACES, YOU CAN ADD SOME FUN CARTOON **SYMBOLS,** TOO ...
OH, YEAH! LIKE SWEAT BEADS!
NERVOUS
AND THOSE BLUSH-LINE THINGS!
EMBARRASSED
THE SIX BASIC EXPRESSIONS SHOW THE EMOTIONS THAT COME FROM **DEEP INSIDE** OF US.

"THEY'RE OFTEN NOT AIMED AT ANYONE... WE MAKE FACES LIKE THAT, EVEN WHEN NO ONE IS AROUND TO SEE THEM."
Sniff
FROWN
FROWN
PURE EXPRESSIONS ARE **SYMMETRICAL** -- THE SAME ON BOTH SIDES.
BUT ...
WHEN **BODY LANGUAGE** GETS INVOLVED, THINGS CAN GET KINDA TILT-Y.
SO WHAT **IS** "BODY LANGUAGE"?
LYNDA? TAKE IT AWAY!
MMPH!

OKAY. BODY LANGUAGE. I USUALLY JUST CALL THEM **POSES** ...
IT'S LIKE...
YOUR BODY MAKES THESE **SHAPES** THAT SHOW HOW YOU FEEL.
LIKE IF YOU FEEL **PROUD** OR **STRONG** ...
YOU MIGHT STAND TALLER, LIKE THIS!
BUT IF YOU'RE FEELING BAD ABOUT YOURSELF, OR WEAK...
YOU MIGHT MAKE YOURSELF SHORTER AND BENT DOWN.

UP AND **DOWN** ARE SYMBOLS EVERYBODY UNDERSTANDS.
THEY CAN EVEN WORK WITH JUST A **PART** OF YOUR BODY, LIKE A CHIN!
ART, YOU'RE TOP OF YOUR CLASS!
OF COURSE!
OH, SORRY, I MEANT BOTTOM.
flip
AM I EXPLAINING THIS OKAY? DID ANY OF THAT MAKE SENSE?
YES! KEEP GOING!

SAME IDEA FOR **IN** AND **OUT.** WHEN YOU FEEL GOOD ABOUT YOURSELF, YOU CAN APPEAR TO **EXPAND.**
WHEN YOU FEEL BAD ABOUT YOURSELF, YOU SORT OF **SHRINK.**
NOW TELL THEM ABOUT THE "BUBBLE."
OKAY.
SO, EVERYONE HAS, LIKE, A BUBBLE OF SPACE THAT THEY FEEL OKAY IN, AND IT GROWS OR SHRINKS WITH DIFFERENT PEOPLE.
WITH STRANGERS, YOU WANT A LOT OF SPACE, SO, **BIG** BUBBLE.

LESS SPACE WITH FRIENDS ...
EVEN LESS SPACE WITH FAMILY -- OR MAYBE NONE!
DEPENDS ON THE FAMILY ...
THIS IS SIMILAR TO THE IDEA OF "PERSONAL SPACE."
I GUESS!
ANOTHER WAY WE SHOW OUR FEELINGS IS HOW **CLOSE** OR **FAR** WE ARE TO EACH OTHER ...
AND THAT GIVES YOU MORE COOL WAYS TO DRAW POSES.

"LIKE HOW PEOPLE LEAN TOWARD OR AWAY FROM SOMEONE DEPENDING ON HOW MUCH THEY LIKE WHAT THEY'RE HEARING."
ART, DO YOU WANT TO GO TO THE SCIENCE MUSEUM AND SEE THE NEW DINOSAUR FOSSIL EXHIBIT?
UH-HUH. TELL ME MORE!
ART, YOU HAVE TO TRY MY NEW ALL-TIME FAVORITE PIZZA TOPPING, PEANUT BUTTER AND ANCHOVIES!
UH-HUH. TELL ME MORE.
AND WE CAN SHOW IT WITH JUST PARTS OF OUR BODIES, TOO.
LIKE TURNING A HEAD AWAY.
OR GIVING A "COLD SHOULDER."

OR CROSSING YOUR ARMS, LIKE THERE'S A WALL BETWEEN YOU AND THE OTHER PERSON BECAUSE THEY'RE JUST SO WRONG, WRONG, WRONG!!
HA HA! SORRY, ART! I DON'T MEAN **YOU** . . .
HA HA!
AND THEN THERE'S THE **TILT-Y** STUFF WHERE YOU MAKE YOUR BODY GO **CROOKED.**
LIKE YOUR BODY IS SAYING, "HEY, SOMETHING IS WEIRD . . . UNBALANCED . . . BENT OUT OF SHAPE."

ANYWAY, THAT'S **BODY LANGUAGE,** I THINK.
UP AND DOWN.
IN AND OUT.
CLOSE AND FAR.
PSST PSST.
AND, UM, TILT-Y!

DRAWING SOME KINDS OF FEELINGS MIGHT MEAN MIXING IN BOTH FACIAL EXPRESSIONS **AND** BODY LANGUAGE.
OH, SO LIKE . . . HAPPY PLUS "UP" IS **PROUD,** RIGHT?
YUP!
AH. AND SAD PLUS "DOWN" IS **ASHAMED.**
AND LIKE WE SAID, EVEN THOUGH THE SIX BASIC EMOTIONS COME FROM INSIDE, AND ARE **BALANCED** ON BOTH SIDES . . .
THERE'S A WHOLE BUNCH OF TILT-Y EXPRESSIONS THAT USE BOTH EMOTION AND BODY LANGUAGE TO **COMMUNICATE.**
. . .

SO IF I SHOW TWO CHARACTERS TALKING IN A COMIC, I CAN USE **WORDS** TO TELL THE READER WHAT THEY'RE FEELING...
Blah Blah Blah Blah
Blah Blah Blah Blah
BUT I CAN ALSO SHOW IT WITH THEIR **FACES**...
AND THEIR **BODIES**...
EVEN WHEN THEY DON'T SAY ANYTHING AT ALL!
COOL!
WE'RE ALWAYS COMMUNICATING! WITH OUR FACES, OUR BODIES... EVEN OUR CLOTHES!
COMMUNICATING WHAT WE FEEL AND THINK...
AND WHO WE ARE.

READY TO TRY SOME FACIAL EXPRESSIONS ON YOUR OWN CHARACTERS?
YEAH!!!

AMP UP THE BODY LANGUAGE!
HOW WOULD I DRAW "DEFEATED BY THE FLAMING SWORD OF JUSTICE"?
OOH -- LIKE THIS!
ACK!
OOF!

NOW TAKE A PICTURE OF ME, MAKAYLA!
I TOOK A **VIDEO!**
IS THAT ALLOWED?
IT'S ENCOURAGED!
HAVE YOUR FRIENDS POSE OR ACT IT OUT YOURSELF. TAKE PICTURES. LOOK IN A MIRROR. IT'S CALLED . . . REFERENCE!

HOWARD?
YES, DAD?
WE NEED TO TALK! I JUST GOT AN EMAIL FROM YOUR TEACHER.
!!!
...
BE RIGHT DOWN!

DAD... I HAVE SOMETHING TO TELL YOU.
I THINK I... WANT TO BE A... CARTOONIST.
DAD.
I'M A CARTOONIST.

CHAPTER SEVEN

MMM...COULD USE A LITTLE CINNAMON.
HI, ART!
ARE YOU BACK TO WANTING TO BE A CHEF AGAIN?
ACTUALLY, THESE ARE FOR MY FRIENDS IN THE CARTOONISTS CLUB!
MMM...NEEDS CINNAMON.
THAT'S WHAT I THOUGHT!
Y'KNOW, I WAS JUST A LITTLE OLDER THAN YOU WHEN I GOT INTERESTED IN MAKING COMICS.

DID COMICS LEAD YOU TO BECOMING AN ANIMATOR?
HEH. ACTUALLY, **FAILING** AT COMICS PROBABLY LED ME TO BECOMING AN ANIMATOR!
I WANT TO FAIL AT SO MANY THINGS.
AND YOU WILL! I HAVE FAITH IN YOU.

ATTENTION, CARTOONISTS! THE BIG LIBRARY DOWNTOWN IS HOSTING A COMICS CONVENTION NEXT MONTH!
A COMICS CONVENTION? AT A LIBRARY?!
EXHIBITOR APPLICATIONS ARE STILL OPEN -- HINT, HINT!

I DON'T KNOW... WE'RE JUST KIDS... WE MIGHT NOT BE GOOD ENOUGH...
WHY NOT? WE'RE CARTOONISTS!
OH NO... THE PRICE OF A TABLE IS FIFTY DOLLARS. THAT'S A **LOT.**
MAYBE WE CAN ASK MS. FATIMA TO HELP?
SCHOOL CLUBS DO GET SMALL BUDGETS. I'M PRETTY SURE WE CAN COVER THE FEE, AND PERHAPS A PORTION OF YOUR SALES CAN GO BACK INTO THE CLUB BUDGET.
SO YOU'RE SAYING CARTOONISTS **ALSO** NEED A LITTLE BUSINESS SENSE?
Math!
¥ £ % $ € ¢
DEFINITELY DOESN'T HURT.

FOR NOW, I ENCOURAGE YOU TO APPLY!
MINI-CON
March 23-24
10:00 am - 5:00 pm
WE'RE BACK!
EXHIBITORS: APPLY TODAY!
TICKETS
LET'S CHECK OUT THE RULES ONLINE.
THEY WANT TO SEE SAMPLES OF OUR WORK.
MINICOMICS
TABLE NAME: THE CARTOONISTS CLUB
CREATORS: MAKAYLA, HOWARD, LYNDA, ART
NAME OF YOUR COMICS: HIKARU AND THE CAT, MR. NUGGET VS. TOFU DOG...
SCANNNN...
uploading...

APPLICATION
SEND
Click!
WHAT ARE WE GOING TO DO WHILE WE WAIT?!

I KNOW! LET'S TALK ABOUT THE
MAGIC OF COMICS!!
ACK! STARS!
OW!
UH, **MAGIC?** AS IN, PULLING RABBITS OUT OF A HAT TYPE MAGIC?
Brush
I'M TALKING ABOUT THE MAGIC OF HOW READING COMICS WORKS!
THOUGH MAYBE WITH ONE OR TWO RABBITS.
COOL! WE CAN EAT COOKIES WHILE WE DISCUSS!
ALSO MAGIC.
AT THE HEART OF COMICS IS A SIMPLE IDEA -- PUTTING ONE PICTURE AFTER ANOTHER TO TELL A STORY ...

Burp!
BUT TO BRING THOSE PICTURES TO LIFE, CARTOONISTS NEED SOME MAGICAL HELP FROM A SPECIAL PARTNER.
A PARTNER WHO'S **RIGHT THERE,** JUST INCHES AWAY!
???
THE READER!
!
OH, THAT'S YOU!
HA HA. WEIRD.
HI.

FOR EXAMPLE . . .
LYNDA, HOW WOULD YOU DESCRIBE WHAT'S HAPPENING IN THESE PANELS?
Burp!
EASY. A BUNNY EATS A CARROT AND RUNS AWAY.
DID YOU **SEE** THE BUNNY EAT THE CARROT?
WELL, NO, BUT . . .
C'MON, IT'S OBVIOUS. A BUNNY SHOWS UP, THE CARROT IS GONE!
"GONE"?
BUT THE CARROT IS STILL THERE.
Burp!
NO, NO, THAT'S **BEFORE.** THIS BOX COMES **AFTER.**

HMM... BUT HOW CAN THEY BE "BEFORE" OR "AFTER" WHEN WE CAN SEE THEM ALL AT THE SAME TIME?
AND HOW DO WE EVEN KNOW IF THE BUNNY AND THE CARROT ARE ANYWHERE NEAR EACH OTHER?
AND COME TO THINK OF IT... IS **THIS** BUNNY...
Burp!
EVEN THE SAME BUNNY AS **THIS** BUNNY?
OF **COURSE** IT IS!
RIGHT! THERE'S ONLY **ONE** BUNNY AND IT TOTALLY ATE THE CARROT.
YEAH, STOP TRYING TO CONFUSE US!
RIGHT, ART?
ART?
EARTH TO ART!

DON'T YOU SEE, MAKAYLA?
THERE **IS** NO CARROT.
?
IT'S ALL JUST LINES AND COLORS! EVERYTHING ELSE IS IN THE READER'S **IMAGINATION!**
WELL, THE **ARTIST** MAKES THE BUNNY AND THE CARROT ...
THE READER JUST, Y'KNOW, **INTERPRETS** THEM.
THE READER IMAGINES IT! LIKE HOW WE'RE ALL IMAGINING YOU HAVING LEGS, EVEN THOUGH WE CAN'T SEE THEM!
WH ...?
OR HOW WE IMAGINE **ONE** LYNDA WHO'S MOVING AND TALKING, INSTEAD OF WHAT'S REALLY THERE ...
TWO **UNMOVING DRAWINGS** OF LYNDA, UNDER TWO WORD BALLOONS MAKING **NO SOUND!**

ART, WHAT WERE YOU EVEN POINTING AT?!
AND WHY WAS THERE A **LADDER** ALL OF A SUDDEN??
OKAY, WE'VE LOST ART NOW!
I THINK ART'S SAYING THAT SINCE WE'RE ALL IN A COMIC, WE'RE ALL MADE OUT OF THE READER'S **IMAGINATION!**
AND THAT IMAGINATION CAN TAKE US ANYWHERE!
WE'RE IN A WHAT NOW?
ACK!
!
FOR EXAMPLE ...

MOST COMICS PANELS SHOW JUST A **PIECE** OF THE PICTURE. A FACE, A HAND, A CLOCK... LITTLE WINDOWS INTO THE WORLD.
HI, MR. BOGGLE!
HELLO, MILLY!
IT'S UP TO THE READER TO IMAGINE THE REST!

ARTISTS CAN'T CONTROL WHAT THEIR READERS SEE "OUTSIDE THE BOX."
HI, MR. BOGGLE!
HELLO, MILLY!
READERS CAN IMAGINE ANYTHING THEY WANT.

BUT, LUCKY FOR US, MOST READERS WILL IMAGINE WHATEVER SCENE SEEMS THE MOST **PROBABLE.**
HI, MR. BOGGLE!
HELLO, MILLY!
SURE, EVERY READER WILL PICTURE THINGS A BIT DIFFERENTLY . . .
BUT THAT'S PART OF THE MAGIC OF COMICS, TOO!
SO MAKING COMICS IS LIKE A PARTNERSHIP OF IMAGINATION?
THAT'S RIGHT!
YOU JUST IMAGINED WHO SAID THIS!
IT TAKES IMAGINATION TO MAKE THEM . . .
AND IMAGINATION TO READ THEM!

BUT OF ALL THE WAYS THE READER'S IMAGINATION POWERS OUR STORIES, IT'S IN THE SPACE **BETWEEN** THE PANELS THAT IT SHINES THE MOST!
Burp!
OUR BRAINS LOVE LOOKING FOR CONNECTIONS!
GOT A PHOTO LIBRARY ON YOUR PHONE?
TRY GATHERING A HUNDRED PHOTOS OF DIFFERENT KINDS OF PEOPLE AND THINGS ...
THEN PICK ANY TWO AT RANDOM.
ONE WAY OR ANOTHER, OUR IMAGINATIONS WILL FIND A WAY TO CONNECT THEM!
OH, I SEE ... IT'S LIKE THEY'RE LAUGHING AT THE CUTE DOG!

HEH.
FANCY PERSON IS TOO GOOD FOR BURGERS.
OR THEY'RE A VEGAN.
OH! OH! THE SQUIRREL IS WAITING FOR A BUS!
HA
HA
HA
GYMNAST TURNS INTO A CLOCK.
OBVIOUSLY.
COMICS IS LIKE A BIG DOT-TO-DOT PUZZLE, AND THE READER GETS TO CONNECT THE DOTS!
Burp!

PLUS, EACH OF THOSE "DOTS" IS A MOMENT IN TIME, SO YOU'RE ALSO CONNECTING **MOMENTS.**
Burp!

AND IT'S UP TO THE CARTOONIST TO DECIDE IF THEY NEED A LOT OF MOMENTS TO TELL THEIR STORY ...
FOR THE TEAM
I LOVE SOFTBALL.
YOU SHOULD TRY OUT.
I'LL NEVER MAKE IT...
BE MORE CONFIDENT!
SHE'S RIGHT!
I'M GONNA TRY OUT FOR SOFTBALL!
RUN!
SOFTBALL TRYOUT TODAY
PITCH!
SWING!
MISS!
CAN I TRY OUT AGAIN?
NO.

SAME STORY!
I'M GONNA TRY OUT FOR SOFTBALL!
OR JUST A **FEW.**
BUT HOW DO WE KNOW WHEN TO USE MORE OR FEWER?
I GUESS WITH MORE MOMENTS, YOU CAN SHOW MORE OF THE LITTLE EVERYDAY DETAILS.
I LOVE READING ABOUT THOSE.
ME TOO.
INDEED! ON THE OTHER HAND, WHY DO YOU THINK A CARTOONIST MIGHT USE FEWER PANELS IN A SCENE?
TO SKIP TO THE EXCITING PARTS, MAYBE? OR TO FIT MORE STORY INTO A SMALL SPACE?
YEAH... AND TO LET THE READER USE EVEN MORE OF THEIR IMAGINATION!

CHOOSING MOMENTS IS JUST ONE OF THE CHOICES WE MAKE WHEN WE WRITE AND DRAW COMICS.
ANOTHER IS HOW WE CHOOSE TO **FRAME** THOSE MOMENTS!
SUCH AS HOW CLOSE OR FAR TO SHOW PEOPLE AND THINGS...
OR HOW HIGH OR LOW TO SHOW THEM FROM...
Yoo-hoo!
OVER HERE!
FEE! FI! FO! FUM!
HELP!
AAAAAHH!
HOW TILTED OR ROTATED...
AND EVEN WHAT SHAPE TO MAKE THE PANELS THEMSELVES.
I LOVE SOFT-BALL!!

THE NEXT IMPORTANT CHOICE IS HOW WE CHOOSE TO MAKE ALL THE **PICTURES** IN THOSE FRAMES!
PAINTED ...
DRAWN ...
OR DIGITAL.
REALISTIC ...
OR CARTOONY!
GRRRR YAP! YAP! YAP!
AWW!

AND THEN THERE ARE ALL THE IMPORTANT CHOICES WE MAKE WHEN WE MIX **PICTURES** . . .
WITH **WORDS!**
LIKE CHOOSING WORDS FOR WHEN OUR CHARACTERS SPEAK . . .
HI, ENID.
GOOD EVENING, ENID.
¡HOLA, ENID!
ENID, I JUST WANT TO CONVEY MY SINCERE REGARDS TO YOU AND YOUR FAMILY AND ASSORTED PETS.
YO. SUP?
CHOOSING FROM ALL THE WORDS-AS-PICTURES WE CALL **SOUND EFFECTS** . . .
CLIK
BOOM
Ahem
Moooooo...
SWOOOSH!!
bip!
POP
BZAP!
BLAM
ping!
WRRRRRRR
RING
BEEP
TIC TIC
SPLASH
TIC TIC TIC
KNOCK KNOCK
FIZZ

CHOOSING TO HARNESS THE **POWER** OF WORDS, AS DEMONSTRATED BY THOUSANDS OF YEARS OF GREAT BOOKS FROM AROUND THE WORLD.
sigh...
LIBRARIAN.
AND ...
"AND" WHAT?
SHE'S NOT SAYING ANYTHING.
OH!
AND CHOOSING WHEN **NOT** TO USE WORDS!
AH! HA HA!

HMM. SO I GET THE CHOICES THING, BUT THE SPACE AND TIME STUFF IS JUST SO WEIRD.
I CAN EXPLAIN! IF THIS PANEL OF ME IS **NOW,** THEN THAT PANEL OF YOU LOOKING CONFUSED IS IN THE **PAST** ...
WHILE **THAT** PANEL OF YOU ABOUT TO FIGURE IT OUT IS IN THE **FUTURE.**
...
OH. I FIGURED IT OUT!
AUGH! WHY IS THERE A LIGHT BULB OVER YOUR HEAD?!
WE'RE IN A COMICS PAGE **RIGHT NOW!**
AND THERE ARE PANELS **EVERYWHERE!**
WHOA ...

HEY, I NEVER NOTICED HOW **MANY** OF US THERE ARE!
OH YEAH. WE'RE ALL OVER THE PLACE.
THAT GIVES ME AN IDEA.
LIGHT BULB!
LET'S TEAM UP!
OKAY!
AND THAT GIVES **ME** AN IDEA.
CAN'T CATCH ME!
HA HA
CLOSE-UP OF ME BEING AN EVIL GENIUS.
AND NOW **PULL BACK** . . .
TO A **LONG SHOT!**
EEK! A GIANT MEEEEE!
HA HA

RRAHHHR!
HELP!
HELP ME, MAKAYLAS!
HA HA HA
STOP, HOWARD!
LET GO OF HOWARD, YOU HOWARD!
SO MANY PANELS . . .
OH, HI, DOWN THERE.
HI, UP THERE.
HI, READER!

HA
HA
WOO-HOO!
HMM...
HELLO?
IS ANYBODY BACK THERE?
HELLO?

YOU FOUND IT!
DO YOU KNOW WHERE YOU ARE?
I THINK SO. YES.
I FOUND THE **BLANK PAGE!**

I LIKE IT HERE.
SO MANY POSSIBILITIES.

I'VE ALWAYS LOVED BLANK PAGES.
WHEN I WAS YOUR AGE, A NEW SKETCHBOOK WAS MORE PRECIOUS THAN GOLD TO ME.
I WANT MY WHOLE WORLD TO FEEL LIKE THIS.
I HOPE IT ALWAYS WILL FOR YOU . . .
THERE YOU ARE!

WE HAD TO GO THROUGH SO MANY PANELS TO FIND YOU. SHEESH!
LYNDA GOT LOST IN SOME KIND OF CRISSCROSS-Y LINE DRAWING . . .
I THINK IT'S CALLED "CROSSHATCHING."
AND I LIKED IT!
WELL, I'M GLAD YOU FOUND US.
YEAH, WELCOME TO THE BLANK PAGE!
HEY, I KNOW THIS PLACE.
IT'S LIKE THAT FEELING WHEN I'M ABOUT TO FALL ASLEEP . . .

READY FOR MY DREAMS TO START . . .
I KNOW THIS PLACE, TOO.
A BLANK PAGE IS JUST SO BEAUTIFUL AND PERFECT.
I LOVE THINKING ABOUT ALL THE COOL THINGS I COULD DRAW.

BUT THEN BLANK PAGES ALSO KINDA SCARE ME.
WHAT IF I RUIN THEM WITH ALL MY MISTAKES?
WHAT IF THE PAGE WAS BETTER OFF BEFORE I GOT THERE?

AW, COME ON, LYNDA! DON'T YOU SEE HOW AWESOME YOUR DRAWINGS ARE?
THE BLANK PAGE WANTS YOUR COMICS.
ANYWAY, PERFECT IS FOR **ROBOTS.**
MISTAKES ARE WHERE THE PEOPLE ARE!
LET'S MAKE COMICS FOR **PEOPLE!**

RRRRAR!!!!
!!
EEP.
OH NO! WE FORGOT ABOUT GIANT HOWARD AND THE MULTIPLE MAKAYLAS!
!
!
CRASH!
HA HA
HA
HA
HA HA
HA HA HA HA
STOP HIM, MAKAYLAS!
LYNDA, HELP US!
COMING!

THAT WAS UNEXPECTED . . .
HA HA
AH, WELL, TIME TO GET BACK TO THE REAL WORLD.
MS. FATIMA, WILL I ALWAYS BE ABLE TO VISIT HERE?

THAT'S UP TO YOU.
SOME PEOPLE FORGET HOW TO SEE THE BLANK PAGE WHEN THEY GET OLDER.
THEIR PAGES BECOME HALF FILLED IN ALREADY WITH ALL THE THINGS THEY THINK THEY KNOW.
I DON'T **EVER** WANT TO FORGET.

I WANT TO KEEP SEEING POSSIBILITIES.
I WANT TO KEEP LEARNING NEW THINGS.

...AND THAT'S THE MAGIC OF COMICS! SEE YOU ALL NEXT WEEK, AND THANKS TO EVERYONE WHO BROUGHT SNACKS!
MMM... CARROTS.
MMM... COOKIES.
MMM... COMICS!
I CAN TELL WHAT YOU'RE THINKING, HOWARD. AND, NO, I DON'T WANT THE LAST COOKIE.
REALLY? ARE YOU SURE?
OH, JUST DO IT.

HI, DAD!
HEY, BUD!
BUCKLE UP!
GASP!
WAIT A SEC.
??

FATIMA? IS THAT YOU?
IT'S BEEN AGES!
RICHARD?!

HANG ON ... YOU TWO **KNOW** EACH OTHER?
Blah Blah
Blah
Blah
Blah
YES INDEED.

WHEN WE WERE TEENAGERS, FATIMA AND I WOULD HANG OUT WITH FRIENDS AT A FUN LOCAL COMICS CONVENTION.
THEY USED TO HOST IT AT A BIG LIBRARY NEARBY.
NOT JUST **USED TO . . .**
THEY'RE DOING IT AGAIN THIS YEAR!
YEAH, HERE'S THE PERMISSION SLIP FOR ME TO GO. MS. FATIMA IS OUR CLUB ADVISOR!
OH! HA HA. OF COURSE YOU ARE.
YOU SHOULD JOIN US!
YOU BET!
SEE YOU THERE!

CHAPTER EIGHT

CRAFT MIDDLE SCHOOL
CRAFT MIDDLE SCHOOL
03/01 PICTURE DAY
03/14 MATHLETES
03/31 COSTUME DANCE
HOME OF THE WILDCATS!!

TICK
TICK
TICK

WAITING IS SO HAAAAARD!

THE CONVENTION PEOPLE SAID THEY'D GIVE US AN ANSWER BY TODAY... I'M SURE WE'LL HEAR FROM THEM SOON.
OOH! I'VE HEARD ABOUT THESE SCRIBBLY SYMBOLS!
HUH??
ART! GIVE ME BACK MY WORD BALLOON!
I THINK THEY'RE CALLED GRAWLIXES.
MS. FATIMA, COULD YOU TELL ART WE'RE NOT IN THE "MAGIC OF COMICS" CHAPTER ANYMORE?
I AM **NEVER** LEAVING THAT CHAPTER.

MAKAYLA'S CORRECT, ART. BUT YES, WE DO CALL THEM GRAWLIXES.
ALSO, THOSE FLOATING SWEAT BEADS ARE CALLED PLEWDS.
HUH?
WHOA, THAT IS AN **AWESOME** WORD!!
WHAT IF WE'RE NOT GOOD ENOUGH TO GET INTO THE CONVENTION?
EVEN IF WE DON'T GET A TABLE, WE CAN STILL **GO.**
YEAH, IT'LL BE FUN EITHER WAY!
Read

WHILE WE'RE WAITING, DOES ANYONE HAVE ANY MORE QUESTIONS?
I HAVE A QUESTION.
SCOOT
Q:
HOW DO I GET MY DRAWINGS TO LOOK BETTER? IS THERE SOME KIND OF SHORTCUT?
I WANT TO KNOW THAT, TOO.
I THINK I KNOW THE ANSWER.
YES, LYNDA?
PRACTICE?
GROOOOAAN!!
SHE'S RIGHT!

"THERE ARE OTHER THINGS YOU CAN DO, LIKE CHECK OUT DRAWING BOOKS FROM THE LIBRARY."
HOW TO DRAW Animals!
EXPRESSIONS
Trees & Plants
DRAWING HANDS
FIGURE DRAWING
ANATOMY
HISTORIC COSTUMES
Manga Clichés
SUPERHEROES!
Hedgehogs?
"WATCH TUTORIALS ONLINE."
"ASK YOUR FRIENDS OR FAMILY TO POSE FOR YOU! SKETCH EVERYDAY OBJECTS!"
"FIND TRUSTED PEOPLE TO CRITIQUE YOUR WORK!"
LYNDA? DO YOU THINK THIS IS FUNNY?
HMM.
IT WOULD BE FUNNIER IF THE DUCK LOOKED MORE WORRIED.

Q:
IS IT WRONG TO COPY STUFF? ISN'T IT KIND OF CHEATING?
WELL ... YES AND NO.
MOST PEOPLE START OUT BY COPYING A FAVORITE ARTIST.
IT'S A COMMON WAY TO LEARN BASIC SKILLS!
IT'S ONLY "CHEATING" IF YOU PRETEND IT'S 100% YOURS -- OR IF YOU TRY TO MAKE MONEY OFF OTHER PEOPLE'S WORK.
WHOA. DOES THAT REALLY HAPPEN?
ONCE IN A WHILE. OFTEN ONLINE.

"NOW, SOME CREATORS DO **PARODIES** OF WELL-KNOWN CHARACTERS, BUT IT'S USUALLY CLEAR THAT THEY ARE PAYING TRIBUTE RATHER THAN RIPPING OFF THEIR WORK."
IT'S REAL!
DOG MAN
A Tale of Two Kitties
IT'S FAKE!
DOG GUY
LOOKIN' SHARP
IN THE LONG RUN, IT'S PROBABLY BEST TO COME UP WITH A STYLE THAT'S ALL YOUR OWN.
WHAT IF SOMEONE TRIES TO COPY **MY** STYLE?
WE'LL PUT A NOTE ABOUT COPYRIGHT AT THE END OF THIS BOOK. CHECK OUT PAGE 280 FOR MORE INFO!
COOL -- BE RIGHT BACK!

WHERE DID ART JUST GO??!
Q: HOW DOES IT WORK WHEN ONE PERSON DOES THE **WRITING** IN A COMIC, AND ANOTHER PERSON DOES THE **ART?**
I'M BACK! DID I HEAR SOMEONE SAY MY NAME?
UH ... NO?
Read!
PLENTY OF COMICS ARE MADE BY COLLABORATION!
???

SOME WRITERS TYPE UP A FULL SCRIPT LIKE THEY DO FOR MOVIES AND TV SHOWS.
THEN THE ARTIST FOLLOWS THAT EXACTLY. OR MAYBE **NOT** SO EXACTLY, IF EVERYBODY'S OKAY WITH THAT.
gesturing wildly, with small picture symbols in the shape of word balloons coming from their mouths.
and artist might come up with the story just by talking...
"BUT IN OTHER CREATIVE TEAMS, THE WRITER AND ARTIST MIGHT COME UP WITH THE STORY JUST BY TALKING . . ."
"AND THEN THE ARTIST MAKES UP THE DETAILS WHILE DRAWING . . ."
"AND THE WRITER ADDS WORDS LATER!"
A LOT OF THE EARLY SUPERHERO COMIC BOOKS WERE DONE THAT WAY.

COMICS CAN BE MADE BY JUST ONE PERSON, LIKE EACH OF YOU DID WITH YOUR MINICOMICS.
Cheer Up, MOON
THE PERFECT CUPCAKE
"OR THEY CAN BE PUT TOGETHER BY A BIG TEAM OF PEOPLE, EACH ONE OF THEM DOING JUST A SMALL PART OF THE JOB!"
PLOTTER
SCRIPTER
EDITOR
BIG JOB COMICS
PENCILLER
LETTERER
INKER
COLORIST
SEE PAGE 274 FOR MORE INFO ABOUT EACH JOB.

Q: HOW ABOUT **NOW?**
HAVE THE PEOPLE FROM THE CONVENTION WRITTEN BACK YET?
TiK tik tik
NOPE.
NO RESPONSE YET, SORRY.
AAAAAAAAAAAAAAAHHH
whyyyyy
merp.

ANY OTHER QUESTIONS? LYNDA?
. . .
WOULD IT . . . BE OKAY IF I . . .
SHARE MY COMIC WITH THE CLUB?

My Mami and Papi used to love to dance.
yap! yap!
Papi was going to teach me how!
But then...
He got sick.
He couldn't dance anymore.

Mami stopped dancing, too.
And soon all the music faded away.
Everything was so quiet.

I drew pictures of Papi.
Pictures of him and Mami...
Always smiling.

Always Dancing!

Mami works so hard. She has two jobs, so I don't get to see her much.
She picks me up every day after school.
And we ride the bus home together.
LIMITED
It's my favorite time of the day.

I love drawing pictures of mi familia, dancing!
Can you hear the music?

LYNDA, THANK YOU.
OH MY GOSH.
THAT WAS SO BEAUTIFUL.
I HAD NO IDEA YOU WENT THROUGH ALL THAT.
THAT WAS POWERFUL!
WHAT AN AMAZING COMIC!
IT MADE ME REMEMBER MY GRANDPA!
HAVE YOU SHOWN YOUR MAMI?

WOW. UM, THANK YOU, EVERYONE.
COULD I PRINT OUT A FEW COLOR COPIES TO SELL WITH OUR MINICOMICS...
IF THERE'S TIME?
THERE'S TIME.
TO THE PRINTER!

CRAFT MIDDLE SCHOOL
School of distinction
ding!
GOOD NEWS, EVERYONE!
YOUR TABLE APPLICATION TO THE LIBRARY COMICS CONVENTION HAS BEEN ACCEPTED!

AAAAAAAAHHHHHH!!!!!
HOW MUCH DO WE SELL OUR COMICS FOR?
WHAT DO WE WEAR?!
WILL THERE BE SNACKS?
DO YOU THINK PEOPLE WILL COME?
HOW MANY COPIES SHOULD WE BRING?!
AAAAAAAH!!!
WILL WE GET PRONOUN PINS?
ARE WE READY FOR THIS?

CHAPTER NINE

ALL ARE WELCOME HERE
PUBLIC LIBRARY
LOCAL MINI-CON TODAY!
10 AM TO 5 PM

EXIT
HOWARD'S NOT HERE YET... I WONDER WHAT'S TAKING HIM SO LONG?
FATIMA!

JACKIE! HOW ARE YOU? IT'S BEEN AGES!
KIDS, THIS IS MY OLD FRIEND JACKIE. SHE'S THE CREATOR OF ZORA ZINC.
HI!
THE WEBCOMIC? THE ONE WITH THREE MILLION FOLLOWERS?!
WELL, 2.79. BUT YUP, THAT'S ME!
JACKIE, THIS IS THE CARTOONISTS CLUB! LYNDA, MAKAYLA, ART, AND...WE'RE STILL MISSING ONE.
IT'S NICE TO MEET YOU!
omg omg omg omg
omg omg
omg
omg omg

MAY I SEE YOUR WORK?
UM, I DON'T KNOW IF IT'S VERY GOOD ...
BUT ... HERE.
Pepi's Dancing Shoes
WHOA.
VERY NICE. **GREAT** BODY LANGUAGE.
TH-THANK YOU! I REALLY WANT TO BE A CARTOONIST SOMEDAY.
I'D SAY YOU ALREADY ARE!

FIVE MINUTES TILL DOORS OPEN, EXHIBITORS!
OOP -- GOTTA GET TO MY TABLE!
Bye!
HOWARD'S STILL NOT HERE!
YES, I AM! WHEW!
YOU CAN PUT THE BOXES OVER HERE, DAD!

YOU'RE HERE!
HI!
YOUR DAD IS HERE!
SORRY WE'RE LATE.
WE WERE AT THE OFFICE SUPPLY STORE...
PRINTING COLOR COVERS FOR HOWARD'S MINICOMIC!
OOOOOOOH!
YOU CAN DEFINITELY CHARGE MORE FOR THESE NOW!
$1
$2
MS. FATIMA? MAY I SPEAK TO YOU?
OF COURSE.

I...I USED TO THINK COMICS WERE A CHILDISH HOBBY. BUT I'M COMING AROUND.
HOWARD'S READING AND WRITING SKILLS HAVE IMPROVED SO MUCH SINCE HE JOINED THE CLUB!
THAT'S AWESOME, MR. HIRSH!
MYSELF, I HAVEN'T READ COMICS SINCE I WAS A KID.
WELL, YOU'RE IN THE RIGHT PLACE!
DOORS ARE OPEN!!

Crunchy Comics
Crunchy Comics
BEELINE!!

The Car toon ists Club
jackie
HEY, ART. CHECK OUT THE PANEL LISTINGS!
OOH, ROBOT LEGO BUILDING!
HEY, THERE'S A TALK WITH THE VOICE ACTOR FROM THAT WEIRD ANIME I WAS TELLING YOU ABOUT!
EVENTS

EVEN IF WE DON'T SELL ANY COMICS, IT'S STILL FUN TO BE HERE!
YEAH.
THAT'S RIGHT! AND THE FOUR OF YOU HAVE A LOT TO BE PROUD OF. YOU WORKED HARD, LEARNED FROM ONE ANOTHER...
EVENTS
AND MADE SOME GREAT COMICS IN THE PROCESS!
$2
$1
...YEAH.

I'M GONNA GO WALK AROUND.
CARTOONISTS GREEN ROOM
FREE FOR EXHIBITORS!
Chips
KSSHK

SIIIIIIIIPP...
SIGH.
'SCUSE ME, IS THIS SEAT TAKEN?
NO.
PLOP!
MAKAYLA, RIGHT?
MM-HMM.
ROUGH DAY?
KSSHK
MY FRIENDS AND I STARTED OUR CLUB SO WE COULD SHARE OUR COMICS...
SIIIIIIPP...

BUT FINDING READERS IS TOUGH. HOW DO YOU GET ANYONE'S ATTENTION?
HOW DO YOU STAND OUT FROM THE CROWD?
SO NO ONE ELSE HAS SEEN YOUR COMICS YET.
UM, I DO HAVE THREE SUPERFANS AT MY SCHOOL.
THREE?! THAT'S AMAZING!
HA HA, VERY FUNNY.
I MEAN IT! I WENT TO MY FIRST COMICS CONVENTION WHEN I WAS A TEENAGER...

"I WAS STANDING IN LINE TO MEET MY FAVORITE CARTOONIST AND MET A COUPLE OF COOL NERDS IN HIS SIGNING LINE."
"WE TRADED MINICOMICS, AND EVEN THOUGH MINE WEREN'T GREAT ... THEY WERE SO ENTHUSIASTIC."
"I MADE TWO PEOPLE LAUGH THAT DAY."
IT INSPIRED ME TO KEEP GOING, AND THE NEXT THING I KNEW, I HAD QUITE A FEW READERS WHO CARED ABOUT MY CHARACTERS!

MISS JACKIE? COULD I GIVE YOU A COPY OF MY MINICOMIC?
NO.
I'D LIKE TO BUY IT!
OH! HA HA! FIFTY CENTS, HALF PRICE!
A BARGAIN!!
BZT BZT
BREAK TIME'S OVER. MY ASSISTANT SAYS MY LINE IS GETTING TOO LONG!

I'M SORRY THAT I DON'T HAVE ENOUGH MONEY TO BUY ONE OF YOUR BOOKS.
I'LL GIVE YOU ONE! ON ONE CONDITION.
?
YOU HAVE TO PROMISE TO SEND ME A SIGNED COPY OF **YOUR** FIRST BOOK WHEN IT'S PUBLISHED IN A FEW YEARS.
wink!
DEAL!

TO MAKAYLA!
YOUR FAN,
Jackie
BUZZ
BUZZ
BUZZ
WHO ARE THOSE PEOPLE OVER AT THE CARTOONISTS CLUB'S TABLE?
IT LOOKS LIKE...

The Car toon ists Club
JEFF? TRINA? CECE?
WE'RE COSPLAYING AS YOUR CHARACTERS!
I'M THE CAT.

THIS IS ... I MEAN ... I'M ... I CAN'T BELIEVE YOU ...
Sniff
YOU JUST DON'T KNOW HOW MUCH THIS MEANS TO ME!
WHEN IS ISSUE FOUR COMING OUT?
WE LOVE YOUR COMIC SO MUCH!
THESE COMICS LOOK COOL, TOO!
The Co t ists

ARE YOU ART? WHAT'S YOUR COMIC ABOUT?
MY COMIC IS ABOUT GRYFFIN, A HUMAN-DRAGON HYBRID WHO OPENS A CUPCAKE STORE.
BUT THEN THEY GET INTERESTED IN MAKING TOYS, TOO, SO THEY SELL TOYS AND CUPCAKES . . .
THEN THEY START MAKING HATS AND THEN BOARD GAMES AND THEN JEWELRY . . .

AND, PRETTY SOON, THERE'S NO MORE ROOM ON THE SIGN!
GRYFFIN'S CUPCAKES, TOYS, HATS, SOCKS, BOARD GAMES, JEWELRY, SKATE BOARDS STORE
BUT THEN GRYFFIN, WHO GREW UP AS AN ONLY CHILD, REALIZES THAT NO MATTER WHAT THEY MADE...
IT WAS ALWAYS MORE FUN MAKING THINGS WITH OTHERS.
AND THE THING GRYFFIN REALLY LOVED TO MAKE THE MOST... WAS **FRIENDS.**
AWWWWW!
ALSO, THE COMIC IS SIX HANGING CARDBOARD CUBES WITH ALTERNATE ENDINGS AND ALL THE WORD BALLOONS ARE WRITTEN IN SECRET CODE.
COOL!
WHOA.

WAIT A SEC...
WHO ARE ALL THESE OTHER PEOPLE?
BUZZ BUZZ BUZZ

JACKIE HAPTIC HAS BEEN TELLING HER FANS TO COME CHECK OUT YOUR COMICS.
SHE SAYS YOUR CLUB'S WORK IS THE NEXT BIG THING.
The

KID POD
HA HA HA HA HA HA HA HA
CLINK
CLINK
AND THEY WERE SELLING THIS TINY COMIC BOOK ABOUT ORNITHOLOGY . . .
I NEVER IMAGINED SUCH THINGS EXISTED!
ists Club
OKAY . . . EVERYBODY SAY "COMICS!"

COMICS!!
ATTENTION CON-GOERS! DOORS CLOSING IN FIVE MINUTES!
WELCOME, OUR LAST CUSTOMER!
WHAT CAN WE DO FOR YOU?
HI, UM . . . I READ LYNDA'S COMIC, *PAPI'S DANCING SHOES* . . .

IT'S LIKE YOU WROTE ABOUT ME AND MY LIFE.
I KNOW IT PROBABLY SOUNDS SILLY, BECAUSE YOUR DRAWINGS ARE SO BEAUTIFUL, BUT ...
DO YOU EVER HAVE DOUBTS?
She her

DO YOU EVER FEEL LIKE ... NO MATTER HOW MUCH YOU LOVE IT ...
YOU MIGHT NOT BE GOOD ENOUGH?
IF YOU DON'T MIND ME ASKING ...
DO **YOU** EVER FEEL THAT WAY?
ME? YEAH.
A LOT.
WELCOME TO THE CLUB.

BEHIND THE SCENES

MEET RAINA AND SCOTT!

A CHAT WITH RAINA AND SCOTT

1. How do you two know each other?

I "met" Scott through his work! His masterpiece of a book, *Understanding Comics*, was published when I was a teenager, and my dad (who has always encouraged my interest in making comics) gave me his copy to read. It blew my mind! Years later, I became friends with Scott and his family through the larger comics community, and they were just as lovely and funny and smart as I could have hoped.

When I met Raina, she was making her own self-published zines and online comics with a small but loyal readership. Our family loved hanging out with her, so we always looked her up during our travels. Then we watched with delight as her comics found an incredible number of new readers! But she never stopped being her modest, approachable self — and our great friend.

2. Where did the idea for *The Cartoonists Club* come from?

For years, I've been saying that I wished there was a book like *Understanding Comics*, which is a "comic book about comic books," suitable for slightly younger readers. I even said to more than one person that I wished Scott would make such a book! Then it dawned on me: What if we made it together? Scott and I were both at San Diego Comic-Con in 2019, at a party hosted by Scholastic/Graphix, when I approached him with the idea. Eight or nine months later, he called me up and said "let's do it."

...and Raina said yes!! Ha ha. Obviously.

3. Making comics is hard! How do you get better at it?

The best way is to just draw and draw lots of (not so great) comics until you get better! Making mistakes is a great way to learn. I also like finding super honest friends who will tell me all the ways that my comics are confusing, hard to read, or unsatisfying. Even when it feels bad at first to hear that something you drew didn't quite work, it can be exciting to know exactly what to start fixing.

I also suggest reading as many comic books, graphic novels, and comic strips as you can get your hands on. Different creators do TOTALLY different things with the medium, and you might find inspiration where you least expect it! I only read comic strips growing up, but one of the first comic books I read in college was BONE by Jeff Smith... and it lit some kind of fuse underneath me. I started working on *Smile* just a couple of years later. It was a wild and glorious coincidence that Jeff and I both eventually became Scholastic/Graphix authors, and I still credit him as a bright lantern on my path.

4. Are the characters in this book based on real people?

Makayla, Howard, Art, and Lynda are inspired by many, many kids we have met, talked to, taught, and been impressed by over the years. Some of our own traits, quirks, thoughts, and questions have also ended up in their stories!

For example, when I was a kid, I was pretty shy (like Lynda!), but when people saw my drawings, they realized there was more to me than just the quiet kid in the corner. Drawing and making comics really brought me out of my shell, and telling stories about things that happened in my real life was an amazing way for me to connect with others.

Makayla, Howard, Art, and Lynda have qualities that I've seen very often in my real-life artist friends. Every artist gets excited about different things, but among the most common are qualities like beauty, imagination, honesty, and invention; and you can see how each kid has a different relationship to those qualities. I know that when I was a kid, I was always trying to invent new shapes for my art, so I guess I was a lot like Art in that way.

5. Scott, how do you know so much about the ideas behind comics?

Well, there's still a lot that I don't know, but I guess because my father was a scientist and an inventor, he taught me to always ask questions about the world. And my curiosity led me to find connections between comics and movies and music and science and everything else; which helped me improve my understanding of what makes comics special.

6. Was it fun collaborating with each other?

It was scary fun — which is the best kind! Raina and I have very different working methods. I usually overplan things at the beginning, especially panel designs, while Raina keeps things more sketchy and improvised until it's time to do the final drawings. Thanks to Raina, I've been able to loosen up my style a lot, which is good for me!

I wasn't sure if I was worthy. Honestly! Scott is someone I have looked up to for so long, and my mind works very differently than his does, but that meant pushing myself and my own skills in a new direction. It was a blast to see the results.

7. What advice do you have for kids who want to start their own cartoonists clubs?

It's so much fun to find other kids who want to draw and tell stories just like you do, and having something in common like that is wonderful. But there will probably be a lot of differences, too. Everybody has their own style and their own point of view about making art. Be ready to listen and learn from those differences. My friend Kurt Busiek, who's an award-winning comics writer now, convinced me to start reading comics when we were in seventh grade — and we argued all the time! But we're both better at what we do now because of it.

First, check to see if your school or local library already has one — you might be surprised! If you'd like to create your own, we have gathered a bunch of ideas and tips into an online Cartoonists Club starter pack, which you can find at scholastic.com/cartoonistsclub.

GLOSSARY

Caption: The narration box that gives the reader information; usually in the protagonist's voice but sometimes in the voice of the author. Often used to transition between locations, times of day, or other jumps in the story.

Cartoons, comics, comic books, graphic novels, manga: These are all terms for basically the same thing: images (and sometimes words) in sequence that tell a story. The finished form they take (minicomic, webcomic, printed in a book to sit on a shelf) helps to define which term is used. It also helps people like bookstore owners, librarians, and educators find the right readers for the right stories!

Cartoonist: This one is a little tricky, because the word *cartoon* is most often used to refer to animation. Still, we like it best for someone who makes comics (or any of the terms in the previous example). It has a nicer ring than comic book maker!

The fourth wall: When a character becomes aware of the reader, like on page 175. We call that "breaking the fourth wall."

Grawlixes and plewds: Those funny names for comics symbols that the kids talk about in chapter eight come from a hilarious book by cartoonist Mort Walker called *The Lexicon of Comicana*.

The gutter: The space between panels, where our imagination soars!

Motion lines: The lines that show you the path of a moving object or person. In the old days, they called them *zip ribbons*, which is definitely a cooler name and should probably be brought back.

Panel borders: The boxes around each panel. (Unless the panel is borderless!)

Sound effects: Stylized words (not in a balloon) that represent sounds, not speech. Like *BOOM*, *crrrrrr-AK*, *THUMP*, *ding-ding!*, *aaah-WOOOOH-gah*, and *click*.

Splash page: A full-page panel, often at the beginning of a story or scene.

Spread: Two pages that sit next to each other when you open up a comic.

Storytelling: Comics are more than the sum of just words and images — they work in tandem to form a third art form altogether! Storytelling is the craft of pacing, staging, framing, interplay between art and dialogue, timing your page turns, visual cues, and so much more. It really is an invisible art, but when it all works together, it feels like magic.

Thought balloons or thought bubbles: The extra-bubbly ones with the dotted tails that tell you what a character is thinking.

Thumbnails or layouts: A rough sketch of the whole comic, showing where everything goes, including captions and word balloons.

Word balloons or speech bubbles: We call those blobs of dialogue over people's heads with the pointy tails *word balloons*, but some people call them *speech bubbles*. Take your pick!

COMICS JOBS

Plenty of cartoonists complete a comic from start to finish by themselves — some even print their own comics, like when the clubbers make minicomics in our story. But sometimes, the job of making comics gets split into lots of *separate* jobs done by different people. Here's more information on each one.

Editor: Editors do a million jobs, from pointing out spelling mistakes to helping guide the story and art as a whole. Editors can make a big difference, but often *invisibly* to the reader.

Plotter: The plot is the basic series of events that happen one after the other and shape the overall story. Some artists come up with plot ideas as they draw, and the writer fills in details afterward. Or, someone else, a plotter — or a group of plotters, even — might come up with a plot separately.

Scripter: Scripting is when various elements of the story really get nailed down: the dialogue, the captions, the pacing of the panels on each page. Some scripts are more exact, like movie scripts, with lots of explanations of what the artist will draw. Others leave more room for artists' imaginations.

Penciller: Some artists are great at drawing faces and figures or composing panels, but they don't care as much about the final line drawing. So they draw in light pencil and leave the finished drawings to the inker — especially if it would take too much time for an artist to do both!

Inker: Inkers do finished linework over the (sometimes rough) pencil drawings. In the old days, inkers used markers or dipped pens and brushes into real bottles of ink, but nowadays, many people also use this term for finishing the linework digitally. Even though they draw over other artists' pencils, every inker adds their own style of linework to the comic.

Colorist: Color is another important piece of the puzzle. Like inking, the choice of colors in a comic can transform the reading experience! (Comics that are in black and white are great, too!)

Letterer: A letterer places all the text that you see in a comic. Some people use a special typeface, often based on their own handwriting, to letter their comics. Others *hand*-letter their comics: another kind of craftsmanship with a long, proud history. Letterers are sometimes responsible for adding sound effects, but other times the penciller and inker create them as part of the art.

Designer: When taking a comic from the drawn state to the published state, a designer is the person who assembles all the pages in the correct order, adds in things like page numbers and chapter headers, and works with the artist to create the look of the cover. They also shape the book's overall packaging, guiding the selection of the paper the book prints on as well as any special effects that you might see on the cover. They also help manage, along with the editor, all the people doing all these different jobs!

HOW WE MADE THIS BOOK

1. THUMBNAILS

Raina and Scott both sketched out thumbnails, sometimes tackling pages and scenes individually, or passing them back and forth and reworking each other's panels or dialogue. Their styles are pretty similar at this stage! In this example, Raina sketched panels 1 and 4, and Scott sketched panels 2, 3, and 5. Raina writes dialogue pretty big in her thumbnails, and it's her handwriting that you see in panel 4, but Scott's handwriting that you see in the others.

Tools: Paper and pencils (Raina) and Photoshop (Scott)

2. LAYOUTS

Raina took the thumbnails and worked out the final composition digitally, starting with a mock-up of the lettering placement, then adding in the word balloons, then the drawings. The thumbnails had a basic breakdown of the panel beats, timing, and staging, but while creating the layouts, a lot of thought went into keeping things visually interesting, making sure the storytelling was clear, and working out action, facial expressions, and body language. (Raina generally spends more time on layouts than any other part of the process!) She intentionally left space in panel 5 for Scott's art, which would be added later.

Tools: Clip Studio Paint (lettering placement), Procreate (sketching), Photoshop (compositing)

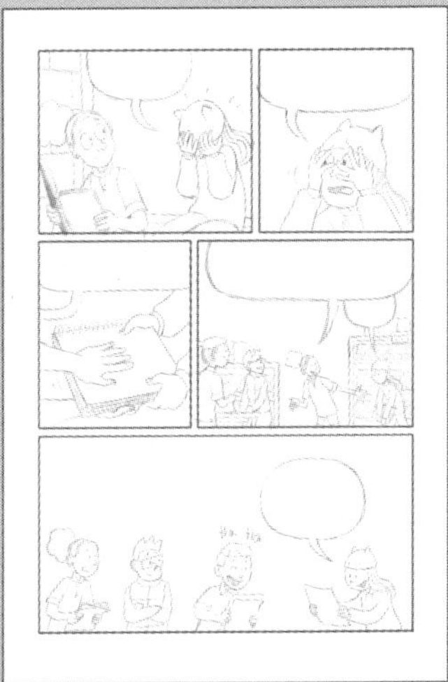

3. PENCILS

Raina printed the layouts on 9″ x 12″ Bristol board in very light blue, grabbed her trusty graphite pencil, and tightened up the layout sketches! Once they were finalized, she scanned the pages and opened them in Photoshop, where she added black panel borders and set up the layers that Ray would be inking.

Tools: Bristol board, pencil, eraser, scanner

4. INKS

Ray inked over all of Raina's pencil art digitally, using Clip Studio Paint! Working on a monthly basis, Ray would send Raina batches of inked files, and Raina would look them over and make occasional, minimal edits before sending them on to the rest of the team. Raina has always inked traditionally with a brush and a bottle of ink, but she really enjoyed having Ray ink her art — Ray brought their own flourish and was really fun to work with.

Tools: Clip Studio Paint

5. SCOTT'S ADDITIONS

Scott created most of the supplementary art in this book: He drew all the comics each clubber made, Makayla's fantasy sequences, Ms. Fatima's comic art, and many diagrams and technical things! On this page, Scott drew all of Howard's doodles that are in panel 5 above the characters.

Tools: Photoshop

6. COLOR

Benny began digitally coloring Ray's inked art with a process called flatting, in which the colorist (or sometimes an assistant working as a flatter) fills every shape on the page that is going to be colored with a "flat" color, meaning there is no shading or other embellishments. After the flatting was done and the colors were just right, Benny added details like shading and colored line art. Benny worked with Raina, Scott, and the rest of the team to establish a general color scheme for the whole book. Every color you see is very intentionally chosen!

Tools: Photoshop

7. LETTERING

Using a script written by Raina and Scott, Jesse placed the text in word balloons drawn by Raina and in yellow narration boxes that Jesse made in Adobe InDesign. First, he centered the text, then he made small changes to the spacing and line breaks so that each block of text followed the shape of its balloon. Words spoken with more emphasis were set in bold, and sometimes Jesse made the letters extra big or very small to show someone yelling or whispering. The sound effects and laughter were all hand-lettered by Raina!

Tools: InDesign

RESOURCES

ONLINE COMPANION FOR *THE CARTOONISTS CLUB*

Join the fun! Create your own Cartoonists Club with exciting games, activities, videos, and more at scholastic.com/cartoonistsclub.

SUGGESTED READING

Adventures in Cartooning by James Sturm, Andrew Arnold, and Alexis Frederick-Frost (Macmillan)

Cat Kid Comic Club by Dav Pilkey (Scholastic)

How to Draw Comics the Marvel Way by Stan Lee and John Buscema (Simon & Schuster)

Let's Make Comics!: An Activity Book to Create, Write, and Draw Your Own Comics by Jess Smart Smiley (Penguin Random House)

COMIC AND CARTOON ART MUSEUMS

These museums feature large collections of original comic and cartoon art and often host great classes and workshops!

THE CARTOON ART MUSEUM

San Francisco, CA | cartoonart.org

COMIC-CON MUSEUM

San Diego, CA | comic-con.org/museum

BILLY IRELAND CARTOON LIBRARY & MUSEUM AT THE OHIO STATE UNIVERSITY

Columbus, OH | cartoons.osu.edu

CHARLES M. SCHULZ MUSEUM

Santa Rosa, CA | schulzmuseum.org

COPYRIGHT

For more information about copyright protection for comics and cartoons, visit copyright.gov/circs/circ44.pdf.

ACKNOWLEDGMENTS

Our humblest thanks to all the talented individuals who helped in the creation of this book: inker Ray Baehr, colorist Beniam C. Hollman, letterer Jesse Post, administrative assistant Eric Langberg, production assistant Hans Lindahl, literary agent Judy Hansen, and the always-amazing team at Scholastic: Cassandra Pelham Fulton, David Saylor, Phil Falco, Lizette Serrano, Seale Ballenger, Erin Berger, Ellie Berger, Emily Nguyen, Emily Heddleson, Meaghan Finnerty, Matt Poulter, Elizabeth Whiting, and Liz Palumbo!

The comics communities of New York City, the San Francisco Bay Area, and the School of Visual Arts; every kid I've ever talked to at a school assembly; everyone I met through the minicomics and self-publishing scene; the Ann Arbor District Library, for inspiring the library AND the convention at the end of this story; the comics shop owners, booksellers, librarians, educators, and geeky parents who help creators find young readers; and Scott for inspiring generations upon generations of cartoonists. **– Raina**

I want to thank my two kids, Sky and Winter, who aren't in middle school anymore but never lost their childlike wonder, and their Mom, Ivy, who we all miss, and who always believed in this book. Also, the kids from my old neighborhood, who taught me what a creative life could be like — and got me making Quanto Comics! And Kurt for getting me into comics when I was in middle school — even though I thought I was too old for them. And of course, the incomparable Raina, who gave the comics world a new and exciting life for many generations to come. **– Scott**

ALSO BY
RAINA TELGEMEIER

BY ANN M. MARTIN
AND RAINA TELGEMEIER

INTERACTIVE JOURNAL

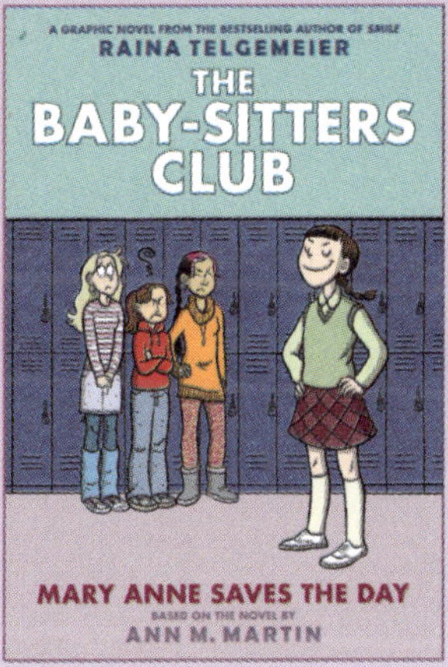

RAINA TELGEMEIER is the #1 *New York Times* bestselling, multiple Eisner Award–winning creator of *Smile, Sisters,* and *Guts*, which are all graphic memoirs based on her childhood. She is also the creator of *Drama* and *Ghosts*, and is the adapter and illustrator of the first four Baby-sitters Club graphic novels. *Facing Feelings: Inside the World of Raina Telgemeier* is based on an exhibition that was held at The Ohio State University's Billy Ireland Cartoon Library & Museum. Raina lives in the San Francisco Bay Area. To learn more, visit her online at goraina.com.

SCOTT McCLOUD is the #1 *New York Times* bestselling author of *Understanding Comics: The Invisible Art; Making Comics: Storytelling Secrets of Comics, Manga, and Graphic Novels; Zot!*; and *The Sculptor*. He is a frequent lecturer on the power of visual communication, creator of the international 24-hour comic movement, and, in 2021, was inducted into the Will Eisner Awards Hall of Fame. He lives with his family in Oregon. His art and stories are available in more than 30 languages and on the web at scottmccloud.com.